MY FIRST DARI DICTIONARY

ENGLISH-DARI

Designed and edited by Maria Watson
Translated by Wasey Wisal

Hippocrene Books, Inc.
New York

My First Dari Dictionary

English-Dari

Hippocrene Books, Inc. edition, 2023

For information, address:
HIPPOCRENE BOOKS, INC.
171 Madison Avenue
New York, NY 10016
www.hippocrenebooks.com

ISBN: 978-0-7818-1441-6

First edition, 2023

Published by arrangement with Biblio Bee Publications, an imprint of ibs Books (UK)
56, Langland Crescent, Stanmore HA7 1NG, U.K.

Printed at Everest Press, New Delhi-110 020 (India)

Aa

actor

bazigar بازیگر

actress

bazigare zan بازیگرزن

adult

بزرگسال / بالغ
bozogsal / balegh

aeroplane
US English **airplane**

havapeyma هواپیما

air conditioner

تهویه کننده هوا
tahviekonande hava

air hostess
US English **flight attendant**

مهماندار هواپیما
mehmandar havapema

airport

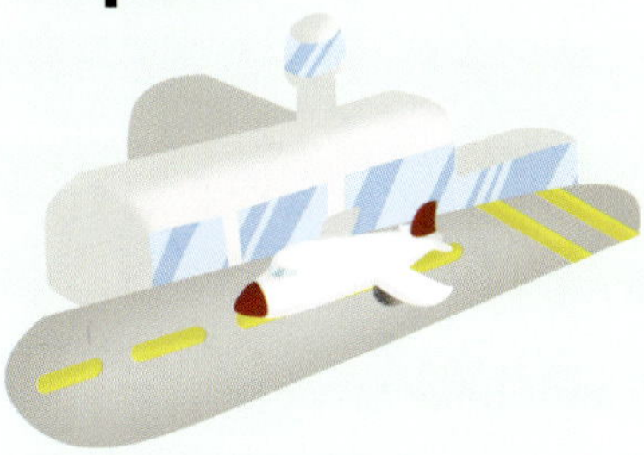

foroodgah فرودگاه

album

albom آلبوم

almond

badam بادام

alphabet

alefba الفبا

ambulance

ambolans امبولانس

a b c d e f g h i j k l m n o p q r s t u v w x y z

angel

freshte فرشته

animal

heyvan حیوان

ankle

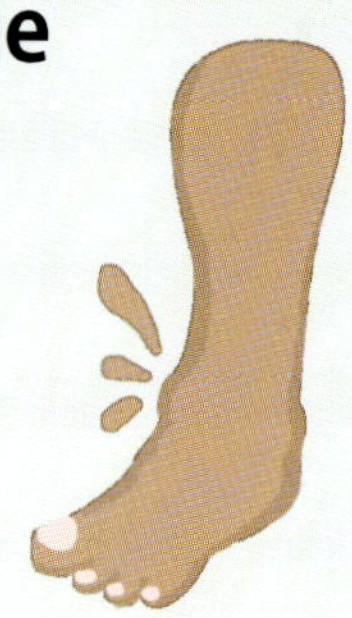

مچ پا/قوزک پاه

moch pa/kozakpa

ant

مورچه/مور

morcheh/mor

antelope

boze kohee بز کوهی

antenna

shakhak شاخک

apartment

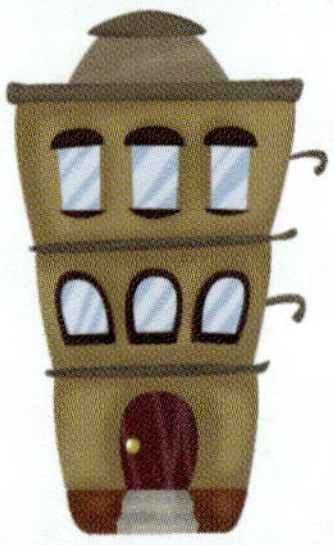

aparteman اپارتمان

ape

boozine بوزینه

apple

seab سیب

apricot

zardaloo زردالو

apron

pishband پیشبند

aquarium

akvarium آکواریوم

archery

teerandazi تیر اندازی

architect

memar معمار

arm

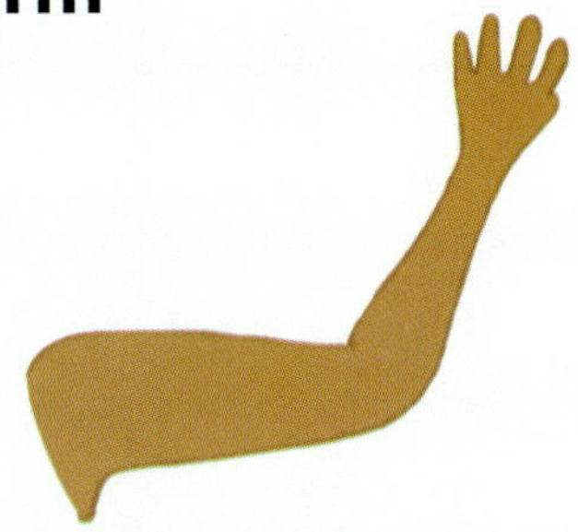

bazoo بازو

armour

US English **armor**

zereh زره

arrow

paykan پیکان

artist

honarmand هنرمند

asparagus

marchobe مارچوبه

astronaut

fazanavard فضانورد

astronomer

ستاره شناس
setare shanes

athlete

varzeshkar ورزشکار

atlas

نقشه اطلس
neqsheh atlas

aunt

khale خاله

a b c d e f g h i j k l m n o p q r s t u v w x y z

author

navisande نویسنده

automobile

mashin ماشین

autumn

فصل پاییز
fasele paeez

avalanche

bahman بهمن

award

jaeze جایزه

axe

tabar تبر

Bb

baby

koodak کودك

back

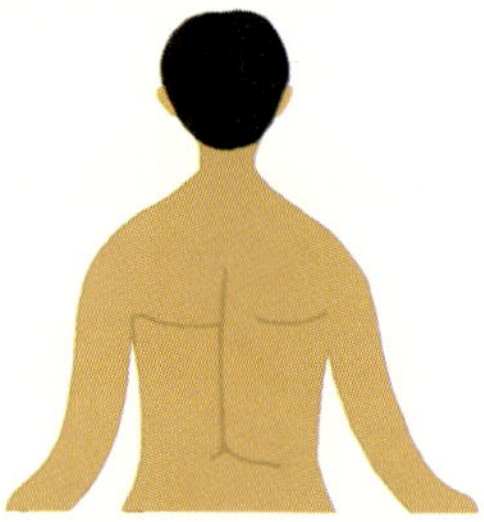

posht پشت

bacon

گوشت خوک
goosht khook

badge

neshan نشان

badminton

badminton بدمینتن

bag

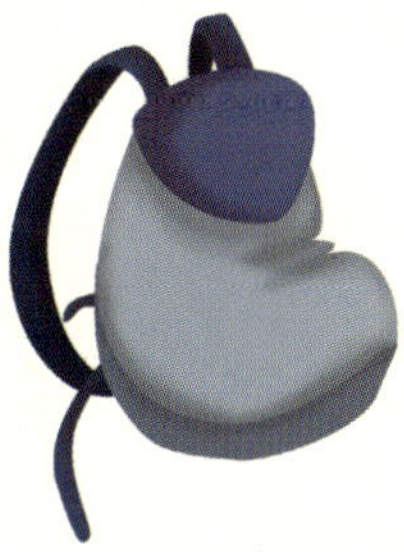

كيف/ كوله پشتي
keef / koole poshtey

baker

nanwa نانوا

balcony

بالكن/ايوان
balkon / eivan

bald

طاس/ كچل
tas / kachal

ball

toop توپ

ballerina

رقاصه باله
ragase baale

balloon

badkonak بادكنك

bamboo

بامبو يا ني هندي
bambo ya nay hendi

banana

moze موز

band

دسته موسيقي
desth moseqhy

bandage

نوار زخم بندي
navar zacham bandy

barbeque

كباب كردن
kabab kardan

barn

tavile طويله

barrel

boshke بشكه

baseball

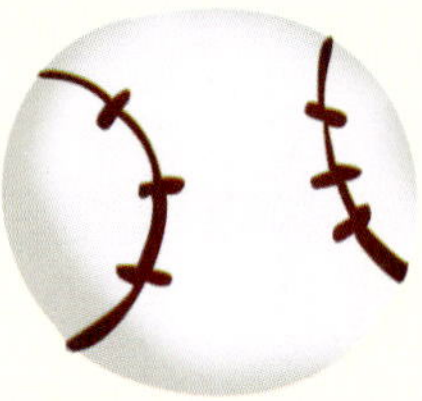

بازي بيسبال
baziey beysbal

basket

سبد يا زنبيل
sabad/zanbil

basketball

بازي بسكتبال
baziey basketbal

bat

khoffash خفاش

bath

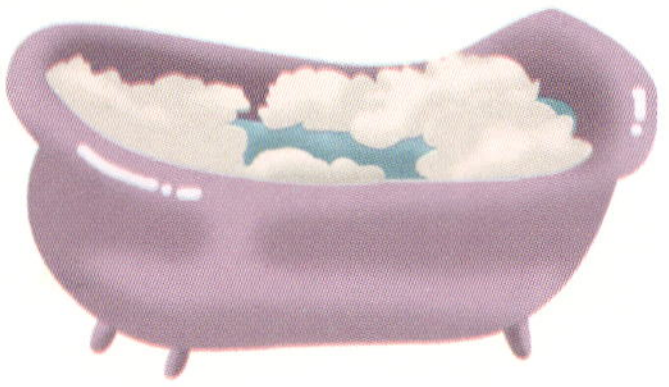

vaan وان

battery

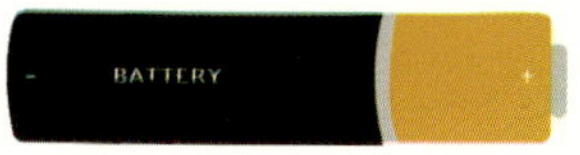

batryh باطري

bay

خليج كوچك
kaleeche koochak

beach

ساحل دريا
sahele darya

beak

menqar منقار

bean

loobia لوبيا

bear

khers خرس

beard

rish ريش

bed

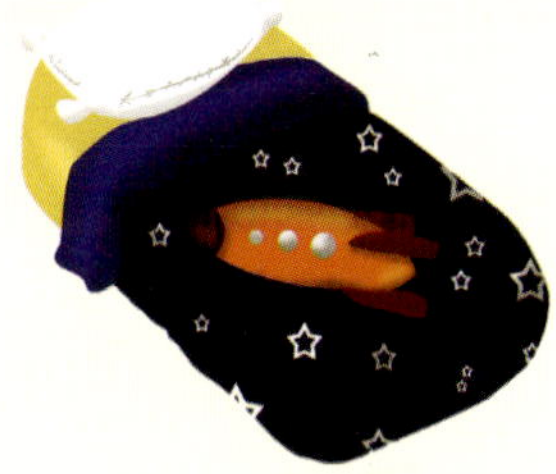

rakhtekhab رختخواب

bee

زنبور عسل
zanboore asal

beetle

soosak سوسك

beetroot

chogondar چغندر

bell

naqoos ناقوس

belt

kamarband كمربند

berry

توت فرنگي
tootfarangy

bicycle

docharkhe دوچرخه

billiards
US English **pool**

بازي بيليارد
baziye biliyard

bin

سطل زباله
satale zobale

bird

parande پرنده

biscuit

kolchah كلچه

black

seeah سياه

blackboard

تخته سياه
takhteh seeah

blanket

patoo پتو

blizzard

koolak كولاك

blood

khoon خون

blue

aby آبي

boat

ghayegh قايق

body

badan بدن

bone

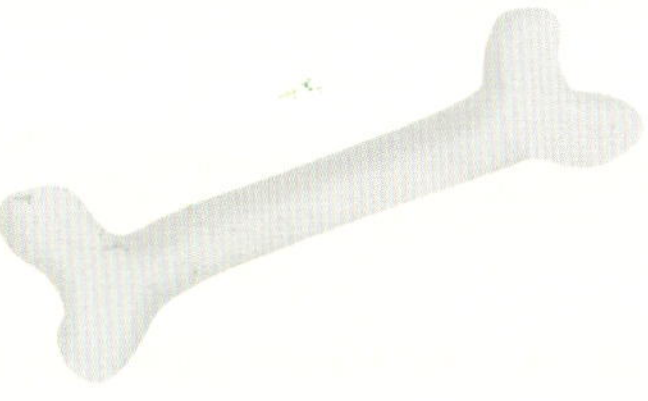

ostekhan استخوان

book

ketab كتاب

boot

chakme چکمه

bottle

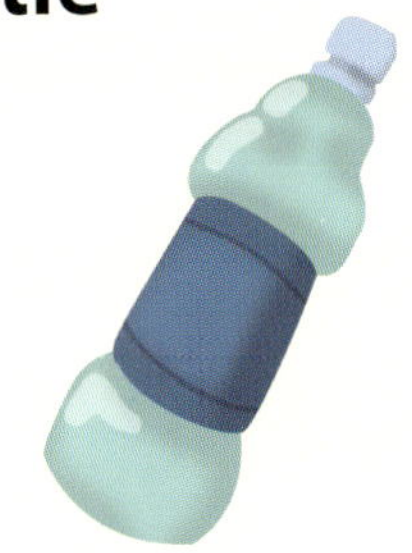

sheeshe شیشه

bow

papeeun پاپیون

bowl

kase کاسه

box

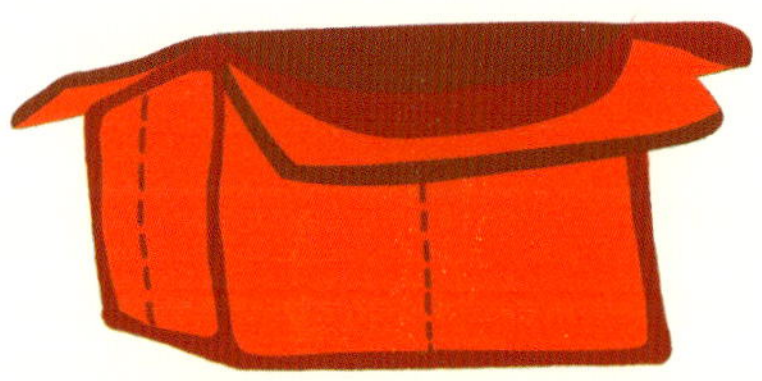

jabe جعبه

boy

پسربچه
pesarbache

bracelet

alangoo النگو

brain

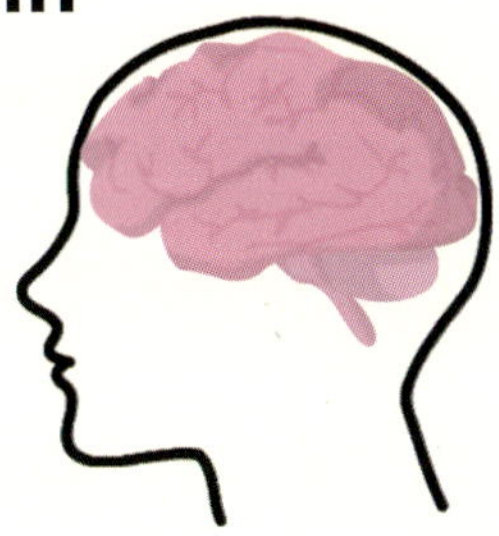

maghz مغز

branch

shakhe شاخه

bread

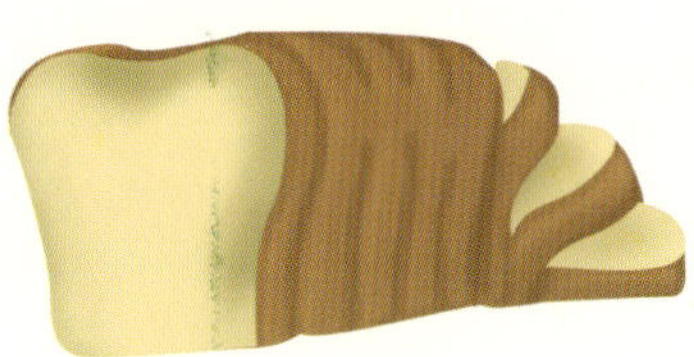

naan نان

breakfast

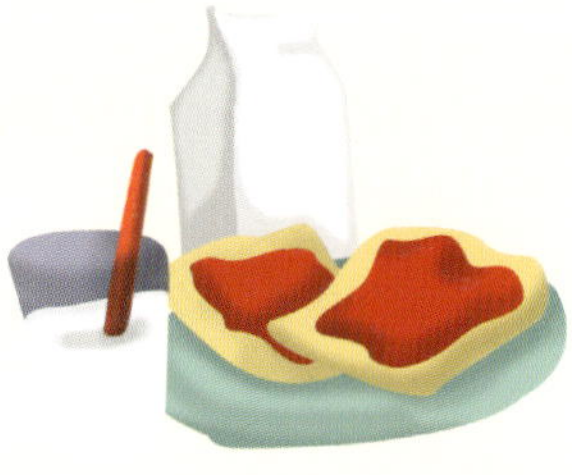

sobhane صبحانه

brick

ehajor آجر

bride

aroos عروس

bridegroom

damad داماد

bridge

pol پل

broom

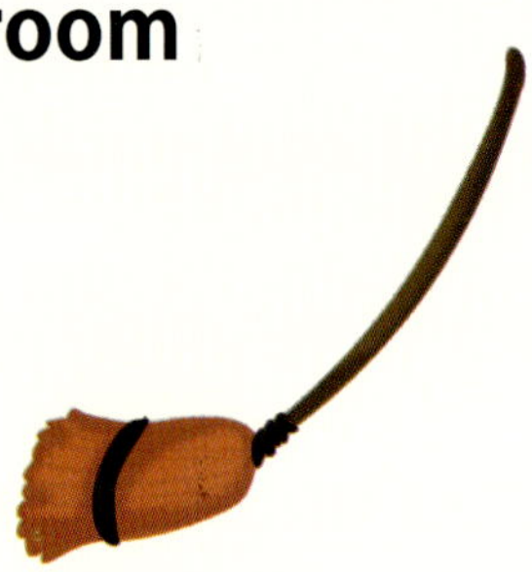

jaroo جارو

brother

baradar برادر

brown

ghahve yee قهوه اي

brush

ghalamoo قلم مو

bubble

hobab حباب

bucket

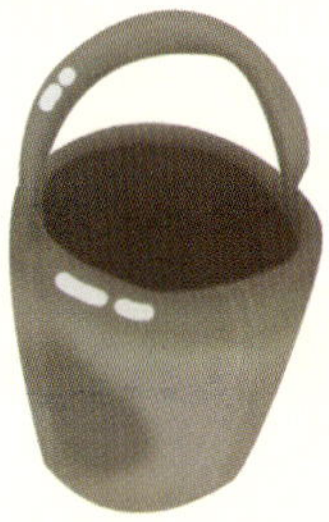

satl سطل

buffalo

گاو وحشي/بوفالو
gave vahsy/boofalo

building

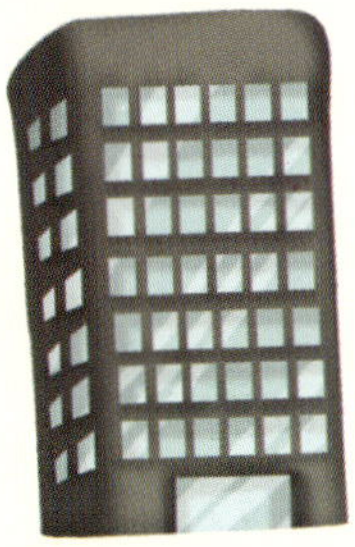

ساختمان
sakhteman

bulb

lamp لامپ

bull

gave nar گاونر

bun

نان کماج
naane komaj

bunch

khooshe خوشه

bundle

baste بسته

bungalow

خانه ییلاقي
khane yeylaghee

burger

berger برگر

bus

otoboos اتوبوس

bush

boote بوته

butcher

gassab قصاب

butter

kare کره

butterfly

parvane پروانه

button

dokme دکمه

a b c d e f g h i j k l m n o p q r s t u v w x y z

Cc

cabbage

kalam کلم

cabinet

ghafase قفسه

cable

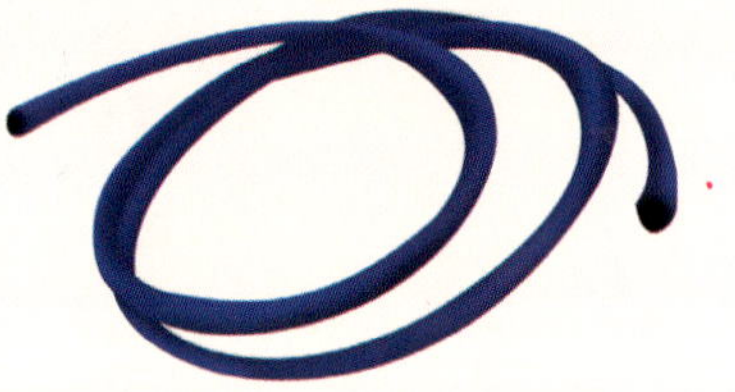

kabl کابل

cable car

تله کابین
tele caabin

cactus

kaktoos کاکتوس

cafe

قهوه خانه
qahwa khana

cage

ghafaseh قفس

cake

keik کیك

calculator

ماشین حساب
mashin hesab

calendar

taqveam تقویم

calf

goosale گوساله

camel

shotor شتر

camera

doorbin دوربين

camp

ordoogah اردوگاه

can

ghooti قوطى

canal

ab rah آب راه

candle

shama شمع

canoe

قايق راني
ghayegh rany

canteen

فروشگاه
forooshgah

cap

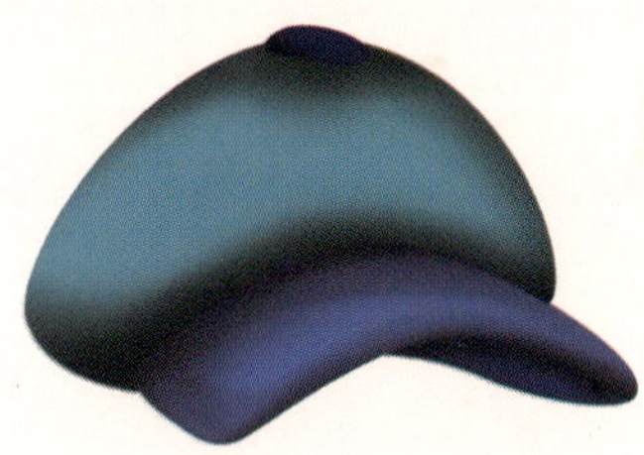

كلاه لبه دار
kholahe labedar

captain

nakhoda ناخدا

car

mashin ماشين

caravan

karevan كاروان

card

kart كارت

carnival

كارناوال/كاروان شادي
karnaval/karvan shady

carpenter

najjar نجار

carpet

farsh فرش

carrot

havij هويج

cart

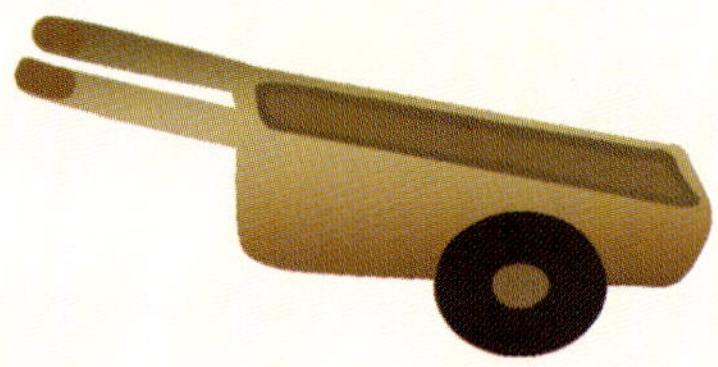

gaary گاري

cartoon

karton كارتون

cascade

abshar آبشار

castle

ghaleh قلعه

cat

gorbe گربه

caterpillar

كرم صدپا
kerme sadpa

cauliflower

gol kalam گل كلم

cave

ghar غار

ceiling

پنکه سقفي
pankeh sagfey

centipede

hezarpa هزارپا

centre
US English **center**

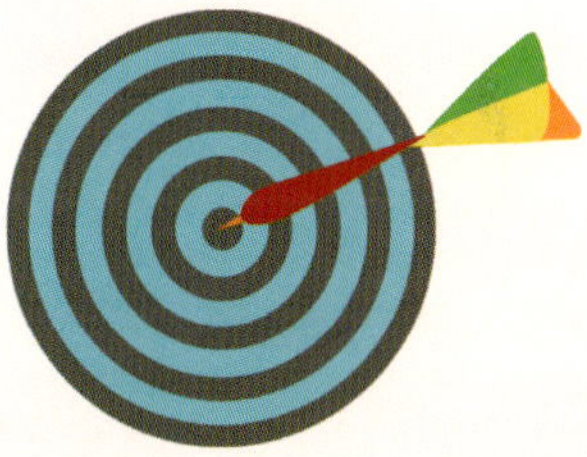

markaz مركز

cereal

ghallat غلات

chain

zanjeer زنجير

chair

sandali صندلي

chalk

gach گچ

cheek

goone گونه

cheese

paneer پنير

chef

sarashpaz سرآشپز

cherry

gilas گيلاس

a b c d e f g h i j k l m n o p q r s t u v w x y z

chess

shtranj شطرنج

chest

seene سینه

chick

jooje جوجه

chilli
US English **chili**

فلفل قرمز
felfel ghermez

chimney

doodkesh دودکش

chin

chane چانه

chocolate

shokolat شکلات

christmas

کریسمس
chrismas

church

kelisa کلیسا

cinema

cinama سینما

circle

dayere دایره

circus

syrk سیرک

city

shahr شهر

classroom

كلاس درس
kelase dars

clinic

darmangah درمانگاه

clock

sa'at ساعت

cloth

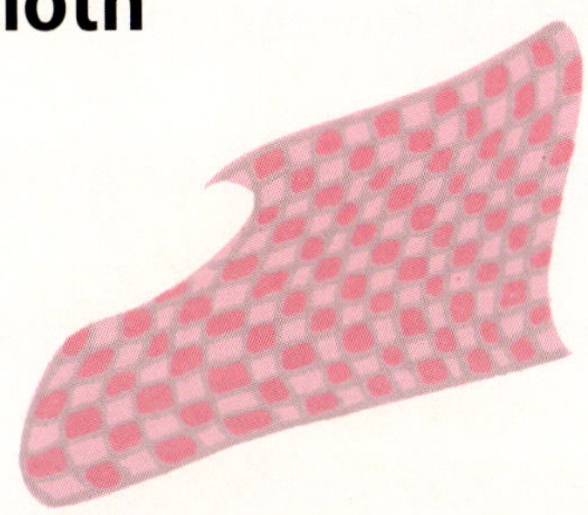

parche پارچه

cloud

abr ابر

clown

dalqhak دلقك

coal

زغال سنگ
zoghal sang

coast

ساحل/كناردريا
sahel/kinar darya

coat

kot كت

cobra

مار كبري
mare kobra

cockerel
US English **rooster**

khoroos خروس

a b c d e f g h i j k l m n o p q r s t u v w x y z

cockroach

سوسك حمام
sooske hammam

coconut

nargel نارگیل

coffee

ghave قهوه

coin

sekke سکه

colour
US English **color**

rang رنگ

comb

shane شانه

comet

ستاره دنباله دار
setere donbaledar

compass

ghotbnama قطب نما

computer

رایانه/کامپیوتر
rayaneh/kamputer

cone

makhroot مخروط

container

zarf ظرف

cook

pokhtan پختن

cookie

شيريني خشك
shiriny khoshk

cord

seame barg سیم برق

corn

zorrat ذرت

cot

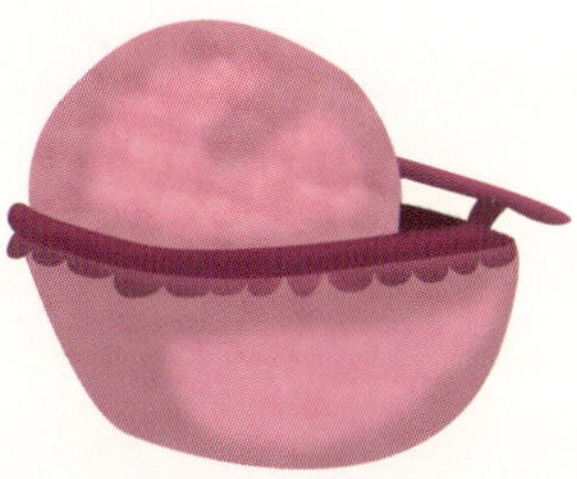

رختخواب بچگانه
rakhtakab bacheh

cottage

kolbe کلبه

cotton

panbe پنبه

country

keshvar کشور

couple

زوج/زن و شوهر
zoj/zan o shohar

court

dadgah دادگاه

cow

gav گاو

crab

kharchang خرچنگ

crane

jaresaghil جرثقیل

crayon

مداد رنگي
madad rangee

crocodile

temsah تمساح

cross

salib صليب

crow

kalag کلاغ

crowd

jameeat جمعيت

crown

تاج پادشاهي
taje padeshahee

cube

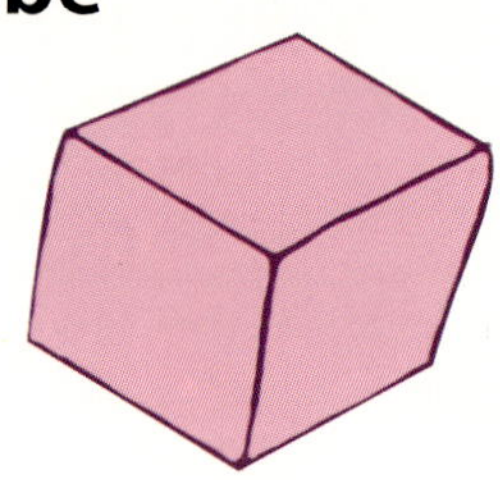

moka'ab مکعب

cucumber

khiar خيار

cup

fenjan فنجان

cupboard

ganje گنجه

curtain

parde پرده

cushion

poshtee پشتي

Dd

dam

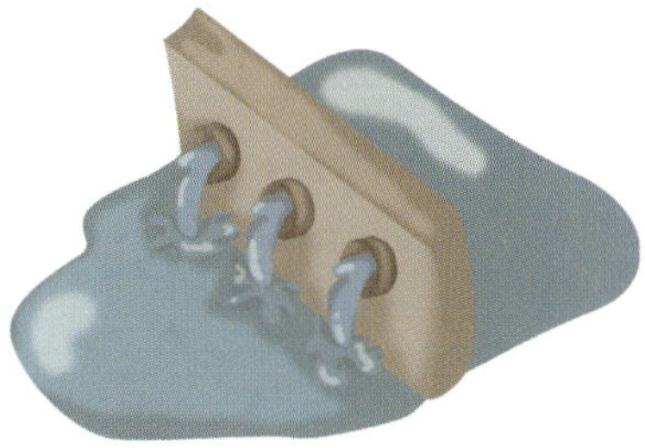

sad سد

dancer

raghas رقاص

dart

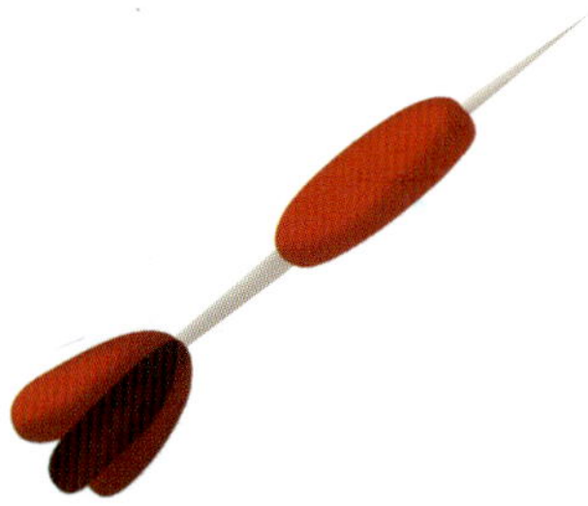

neyze نیزه

data

daade داده

dates

khorma خرما

daughter

فرزند دختر
frazande dokhtar

day

rooz روز

deck

varagh ورق

deer

آهوي كوهي
ahooye koohy

den

كنام شير
koname sheer

dentist

دندانپزشك
dandanpezeshk

desert

kaveer کویر

design

tarh طرح

desk

میز مطالعه
mize motale'e

dessert

deser دسر

detective

caragah کاراگاه

diamond

almas الماس

diary

دفتر خاطرات
daftare khaterat

dice

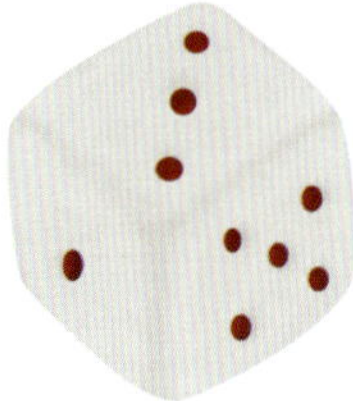

tas تاس

dictionary

فرهنگ لغت
farhange logat

dinosaur

daynasor دایناسور

disc

disk دیسک

dish

boshghab بشقاب

diver

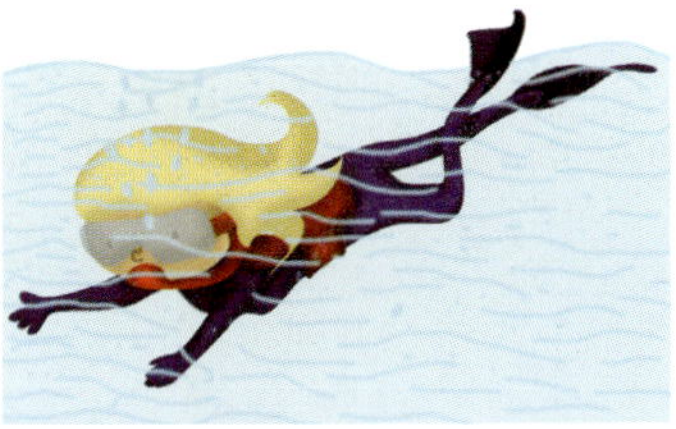

ghavas غواص

dock

eskele اسکله

doctor

doktor دکتر

dog

sag سگ

doll

aroosk عروسك

dolphin

dolfin دولفين

dome

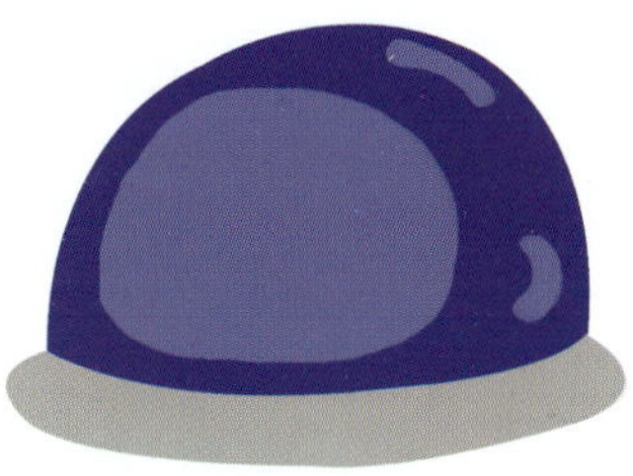

gonbad گنبد

domino

بازي دومينو
bazy domino

donkey

khar/olagh خر/الاغ

donut

donaat دونات

door

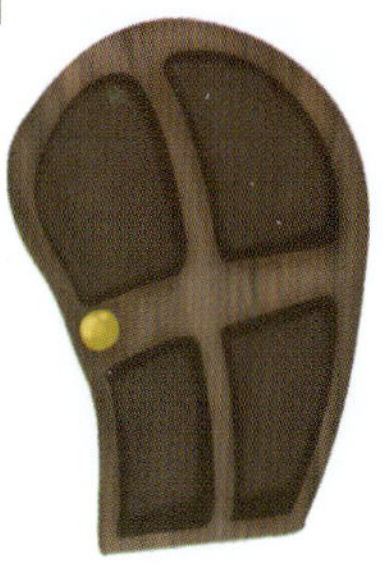

dar در

dough

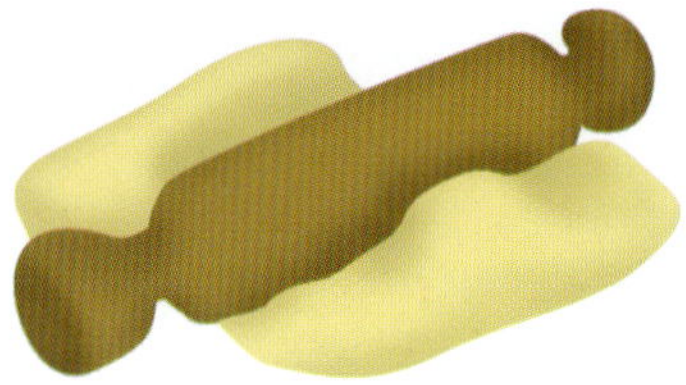

khamir خمير

a b c d e f g h i j k l m n o p q r s t u v w x y z

dragon

ezhdeha اژدها

drain

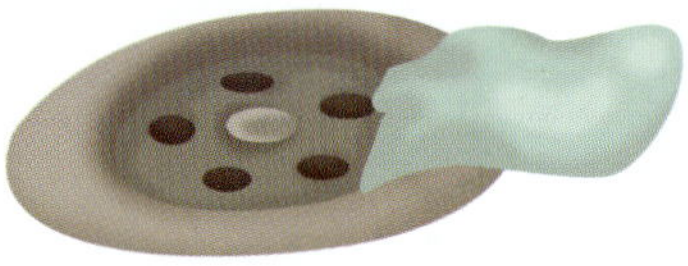

zehkeshy زه کشی

drawer

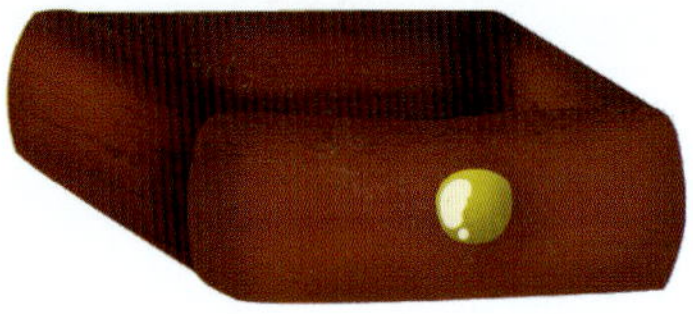

kesho کشو

drawing

tarsim ترسیم

dream

khab/roya خواب/رویا

dress

labas لباس

drink

noshidan نوشیدن

driver

rannde راننده

drop

ghatre قطره

drought

khushk خشک

drum

tabl طبل

duck

ordak اردك

dustbin
US English **trash can**

zobaledany زباله داني

duvet

lahaf لحاف

dwarf

آدم كوتوله
adam kootoole

Ee

eagle

oghab عقاب

ear

goosh گوش

earring

gooshvare گوشواره

earth

zamin زمين

earthquake

زمين لرزه
zamin larze

earthworm

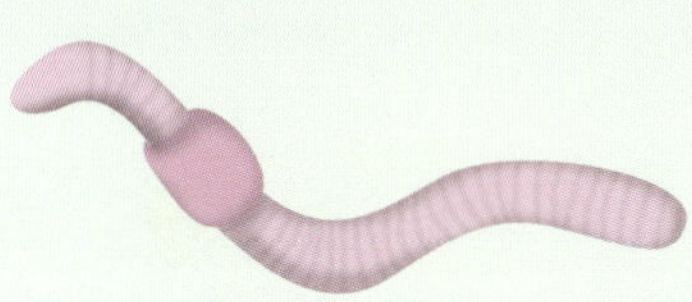

كرم خاكي
kerme khaki

eclipse

كسوف يا خسوف
kosoof ya khosoof

edge

labeh لبه

eel

marmahee مارماهي

egg

تخم مرغ
tokhme morgh

eight

hasht هشت

elastic

kesh کش

elbow

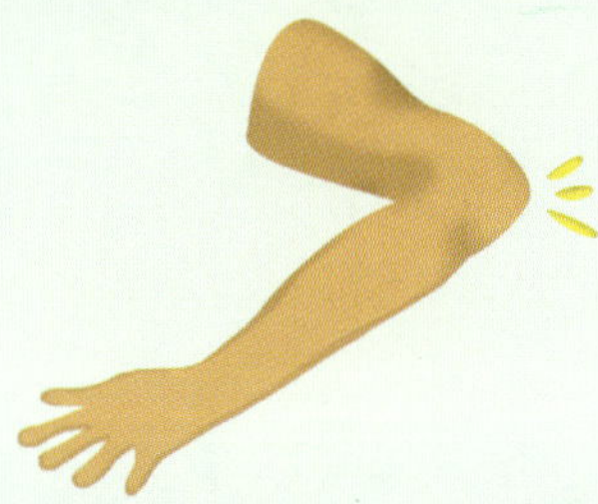

aranj آرنج

electrician

تکنسین برق
tekeesiane bargh

electricity

barqh برق

elephant

feal فیل

elevator

asansor آسانسور

elf

pary پری

email

پست الکترونیک
post electronic

embroidery

سوزن دوزي
soozandoozi

engine

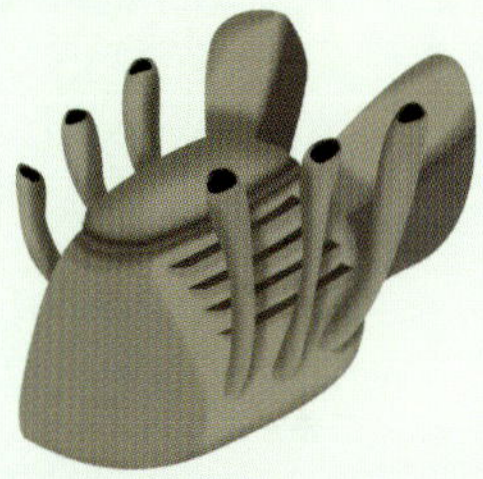

motor موتور

entrance

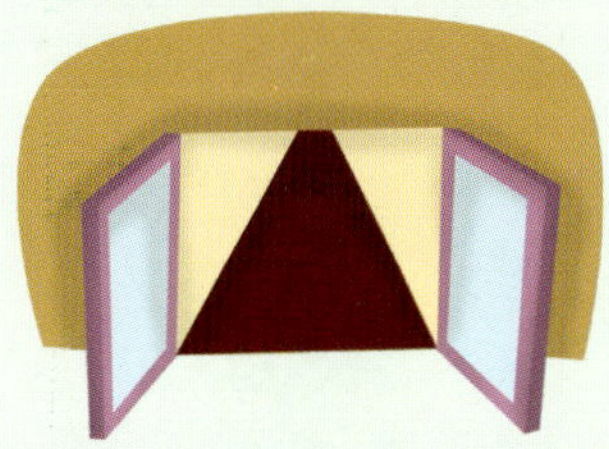

vorood ورود

envelope

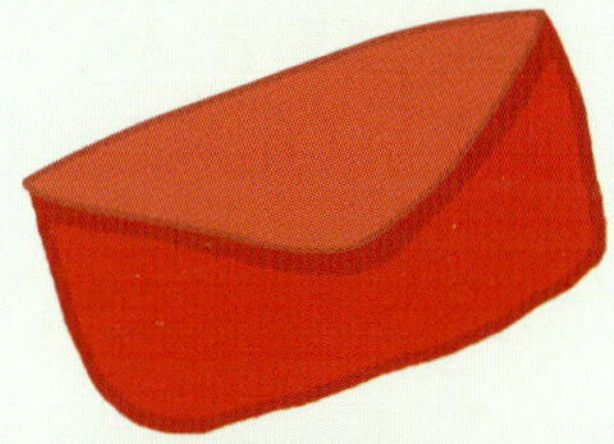

پاکت نامه
pakatname

equator

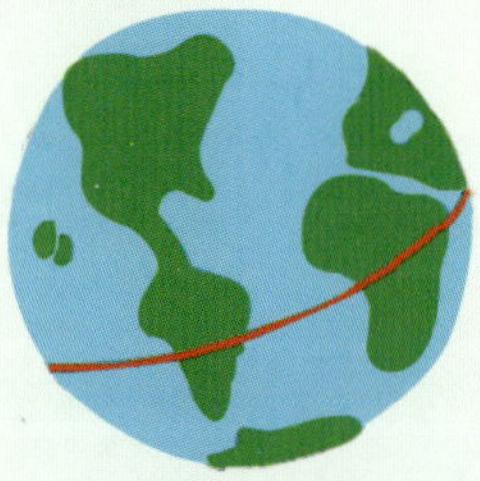

خط استوا
khate ostva

equipment

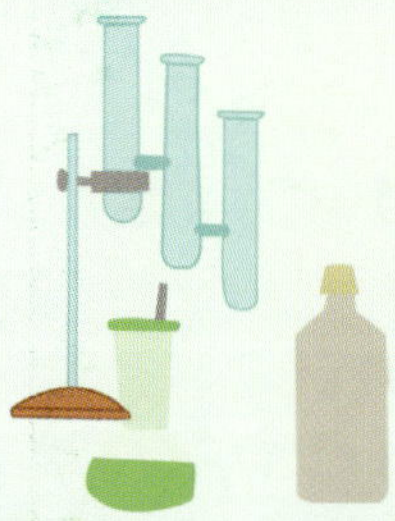

tajhizat تجهیزات

eraser

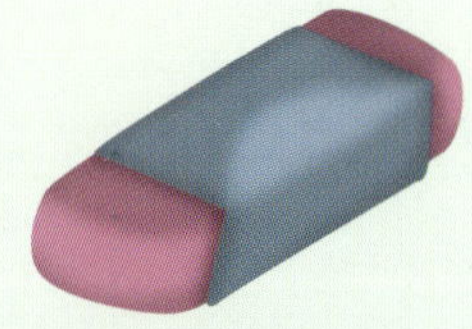

pakkon پاک کن

escalator

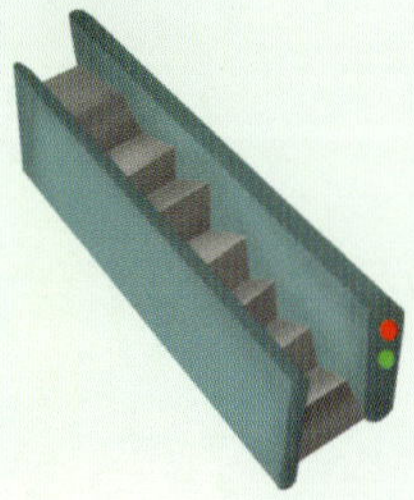

pelle bargi پله برقی

eskimo

eskimo اسکیمو

evening

شب\غروب
shab/groob

exhibition

نمایشگاه
namayeshgah

eye

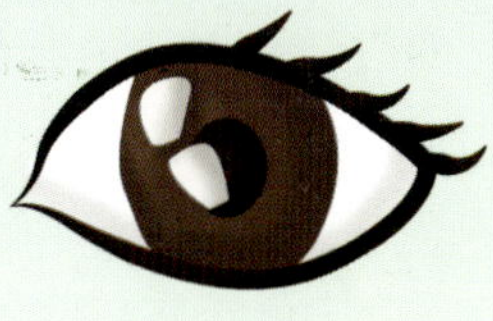

cheshm چشم

eyebrow

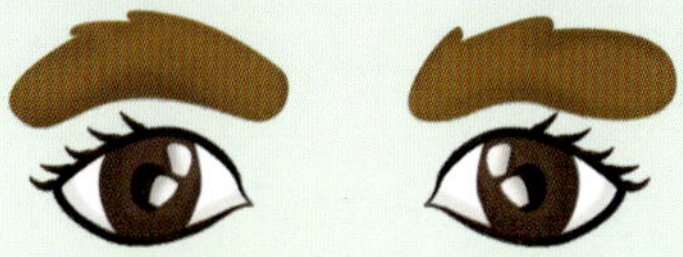

abroo ابرو

Ff

fabric

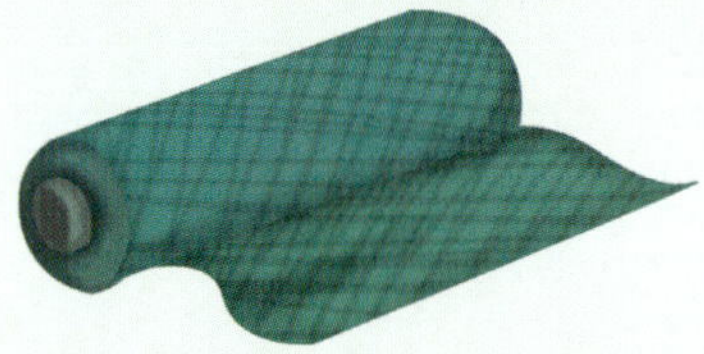

parche پارچه

face

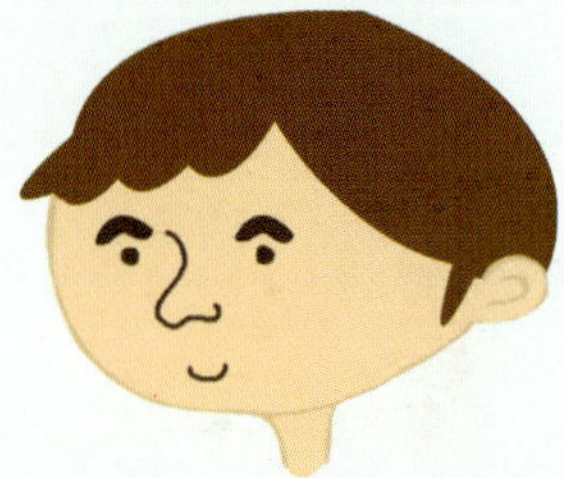

soorat صورت

factory

karkhane کارخانه

fairy

paray پري

family

khanevade خانواده

fan

bad bezan بادزن

farm

mazrae مزرعه

farmer

keshavar کشاورز

fat

chagh چاق

father

pedar پدر

feather

par پر

female

moanas مؤنث

fence

hesar حصار

ferry

keshtee کشتی

field

mazrae مزرعه

fig

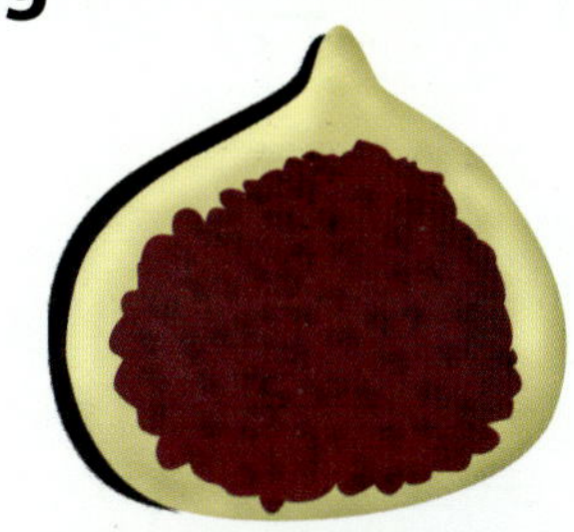

anjeer انجیر

file

parvande پرونده

film

film فیلم

finger

anghosht انگشت

fire

atash آتش

fire engine

ماشین آتش نشانی
mashine atash neshany

fire fighter

مامور اتش نشانی
mamoore atash neshany

fireworks

atashbazy آتش بازی

fish

mahee ماهي

fist

mosht مشت

five

panj پنج

flag

parcham پرچم

flame

shole شعله

flamingo

flamingo فلامینگو

flask

ghoghome قمقمه

flock

galle گله

flood

seyl سیل

floor

kaf کف

florist

golforrosh گلفروش

flour

ard آرد

flower

gol گل

flute

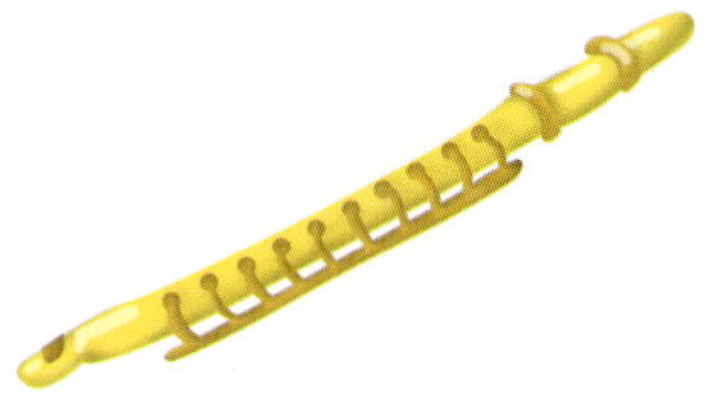

flute فلوت

fly

magas مگس

foam

kaf كف

fog

meh مه

foil

فويل آلومينيوم
foile alomineum

food

خوراك/غذا
khorak/gaza

foot

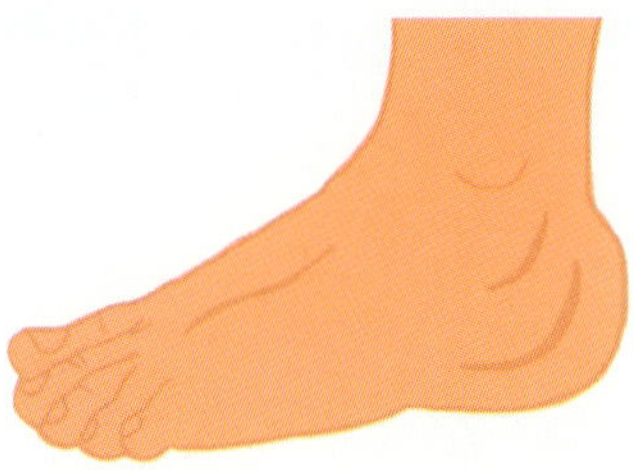

pa پا

football
US English **soccer**

footbal فوتبال

forearm

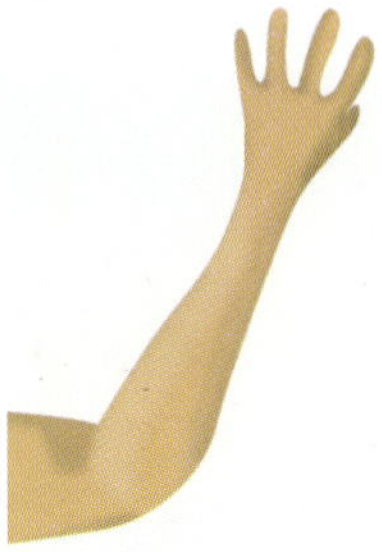

saed ساعد

forehead

pishany پيشاني

forest

jangal جنگل

fork

changal چنگال

fortress

dej دژ

fountain

favvare فواره

four

chahar چهار

fox

roobah روباه

frame

qab قاب

freezer

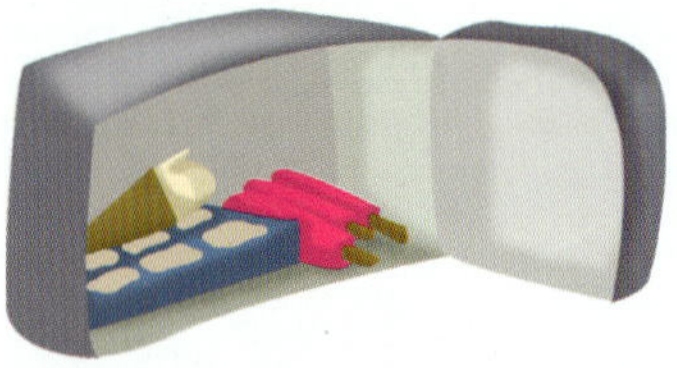

freezer فریز

fridge

US English **refrigerator**

yakh chal یخچال

friend

doost دوست

frog

goorbage قورباغه

fruit

mive میوه

fumes

dood دود

funnel

gheef قیف

furnace

koore کوره

furniture

mobleman مبلمان

Gg

gadget

abzar ابزار

gallery

آلبوم عکس
albome aks

game

bazi بازی

gap

shekaf شکاف

garage

garaj گاراژ

garbage

zobale زباله

garden

bagh باغ

garland

halghe gol حلقه گل

garlic

sear سير

gas

gaaz گاز

gate

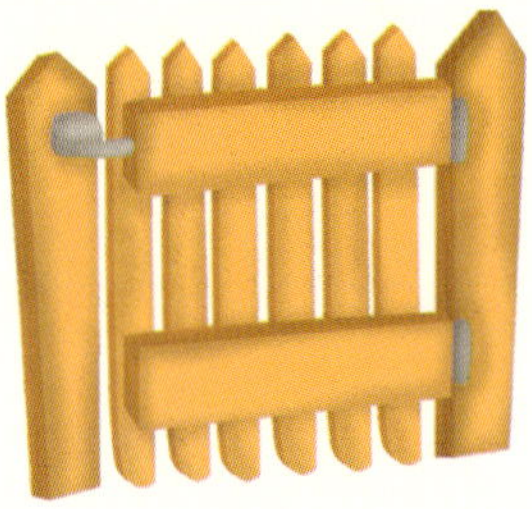

dervaze دروازه

gem

سنگ قيمتي
sang gheymati

generator

jenerator ژنراتور

germ

microb ميكروب

geyser

چشمه اب گرم
cheshme abe garm

ghost

rooh روح

giant

ghool غول

gift

hediye هديه

ginger

zanjebil زنجبيل

giraffe

zarafe زرافه

girl

dokhtar دختر

glacier

یخچال طبیعی
yakh chal tabee'ee

glass

shishe شیشه

glider

هواپیمای بی موتور
havapeymaye bi motor

globe

kore کره

glove

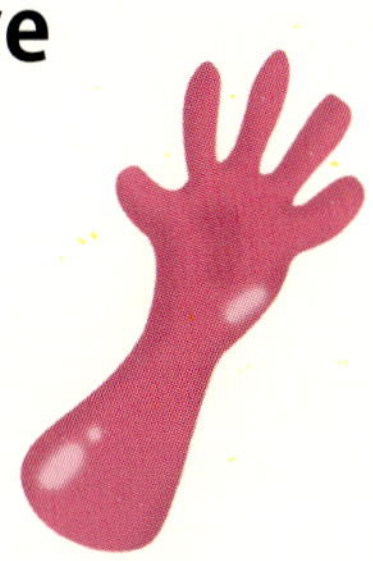

dastkesh دستکش

glue

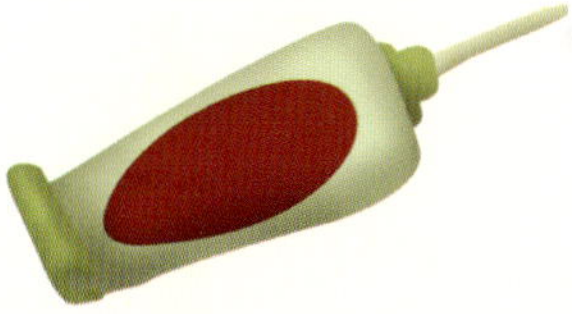

chasb چسب

goal

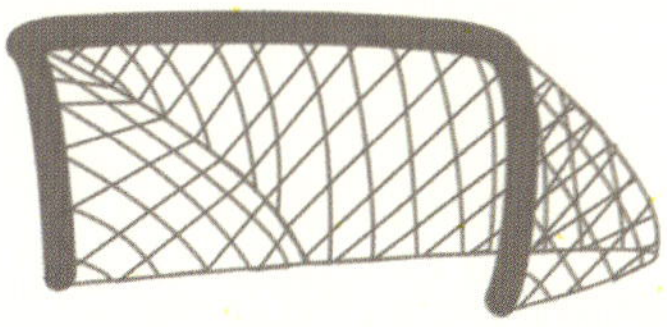

gol گل

goat

boz بز

gold

tala طلا

golf

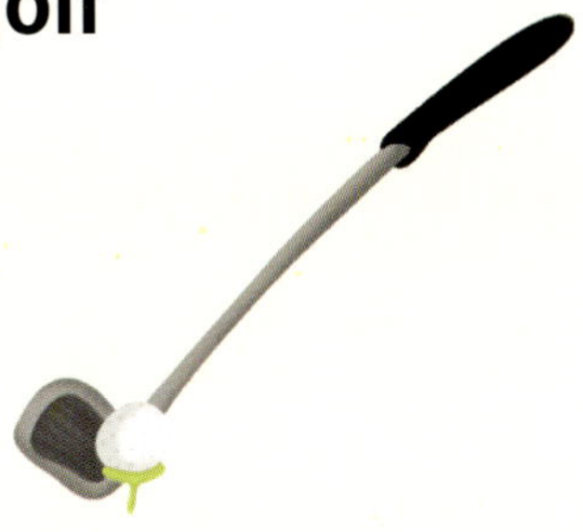

golf گلف

goose

ghaz غاز

gorilla

gooreel گوریل

grain

ghalat غلات

grandfather

بابا بزرگ
baba bozorg

grandmother

مادر بزرگ
madar bozorg

grape

angoor انگور

grapefruit

گریپ فروت
greep froot

grass

chaman چمن

grasshopper

malakh ملخ

gravel

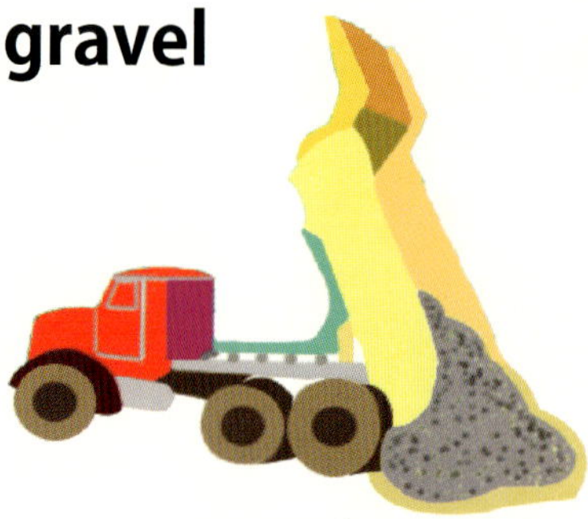

سنگ ریزه
sang reeze

green

sabz سبز

grey

khakestary خاکستری

grill

manghal منقل

grocery

kharbar خواربار

ground

zamin زمین

guard

nagahban نگهبان

guava

guava گوا

guide

rahnama راهنما

guitar

geetar گیتار

gulf

khalij خلیج

gun

tofang تفنگ

gypsy

koli کولی

Hh

hair

moo مو

hairbrush

borse moo بروس مو

hairdresser

salmany سلماني

half

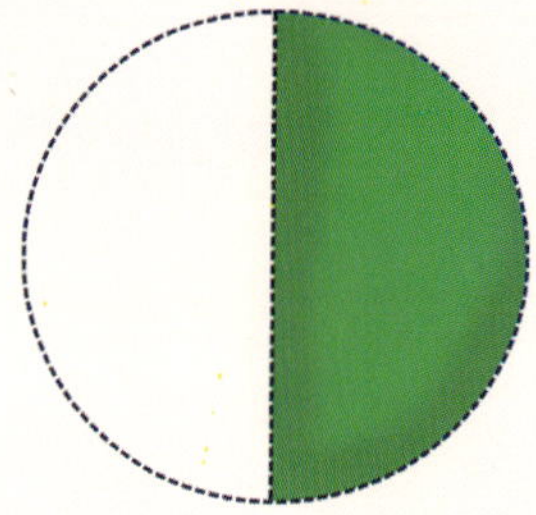

neam نيم

hall

salon سالن

ham

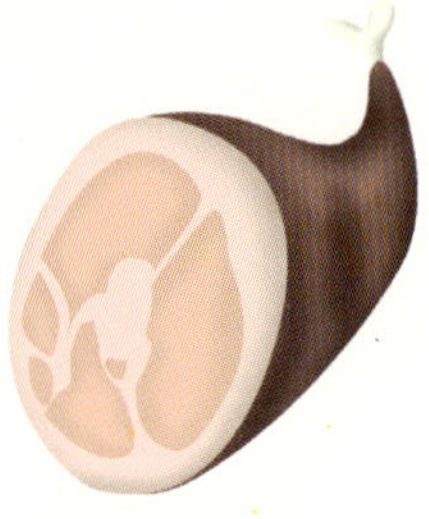

jambon ژامبون

hammer

chakkosh چکش

hammock

banooj بانوج

hand

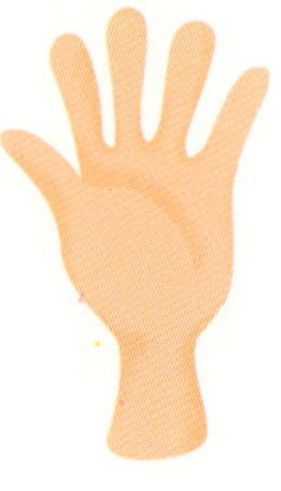

dast دست

handbag

کیف دستی
kif dasty

handicraft

هنر دستی
honar dasty

handkerchief

dastmal دستمال

handle

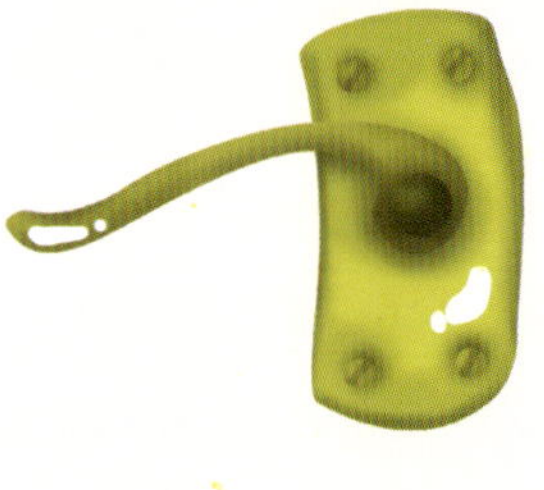

rasedagy رسیدگی

hanger

ja rakhtee جا رختی

harbour
US English **harbor**

bandargah بندرگاه

hare

khargoosh خرگوش

harvest

mahsool محصول

hat

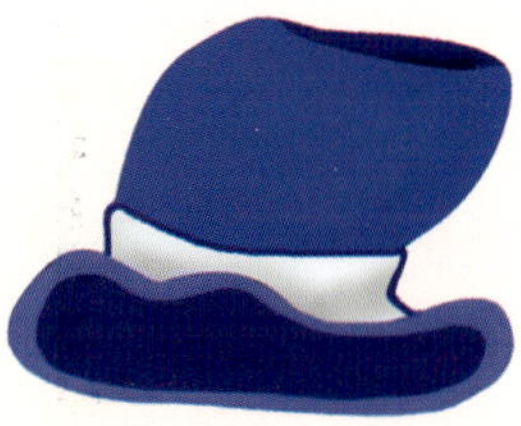

kolah کلاه

hawk

shaheen شاهین

hay

علف خشک
alaf khoshk

head

sar سر

headphone

headfon هدفون

heap

poshte پشته

heart

ghalb قلب

heater

bokhari بخاری

hedge

parchin پرچین

heel

paashneh پاشنه

helicopter

helikoopter هلی کوپتر

helmet

کلاه ایمنی
kolahe eemany

hen

morgh مرغ

herb

گیاه دارویی
geeahe daroee

herd

gleh گله

hermit

گوشه نشین
gosheneshin

hill

tape تپه

hippopotamus

asabe aby اسب ابی

hive

kando asal کندو عسل

hole
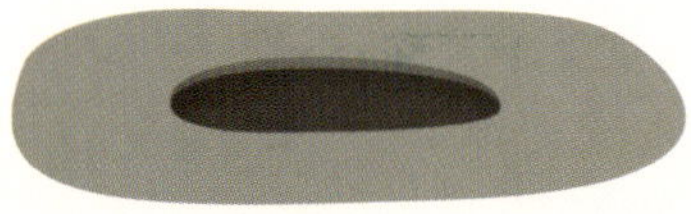
soorakh سوراخ

honey

asal عسل

hood

shenel شنل

hook

ghollab قلاب

horn

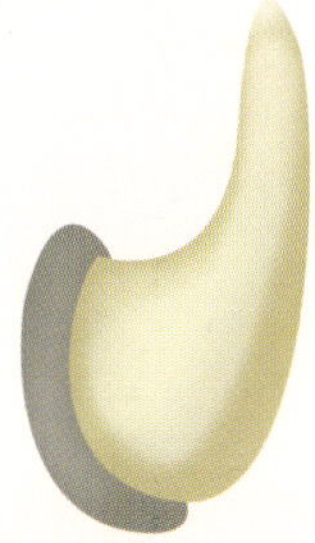

shakh شاخ

horse

asb اسب

hose

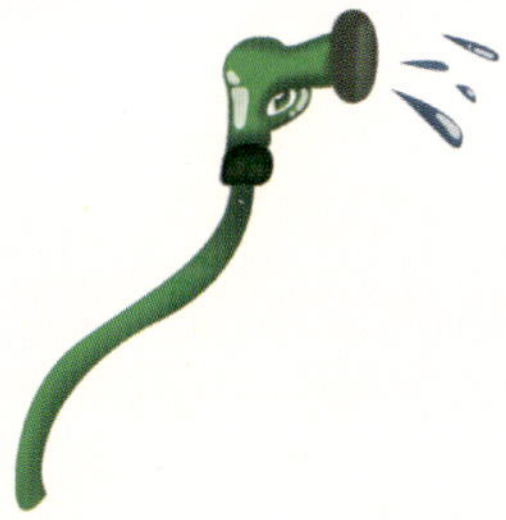

sheelang شلنگ

hospital

بیمارستان
bimarestan

hotdog

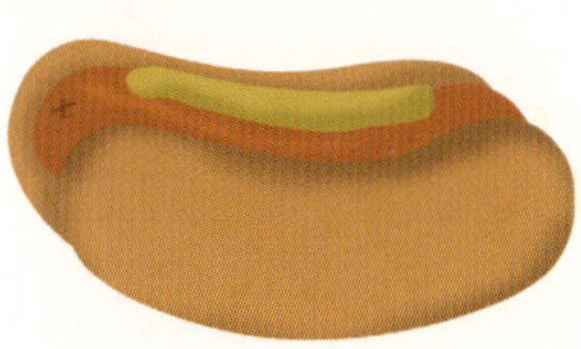

hotdog هات داگ

hotel

hotel هتل

hour

sa'at ساعت

house

khane خانه

human

ensan انسان

hunter

shekarchy شکارچی

a b c d e f g h i j k l m n o p q r s t u v w x y z

hurricane

tofan طوفان

husband

shohar شوهر

hut

kolbe کلبه

Ii

ice

yakh یخ

iceberg

توده یخ شناور
todeye yakhe shenavar

ice cream

bastany بستنی

idol

boat بت

igloo

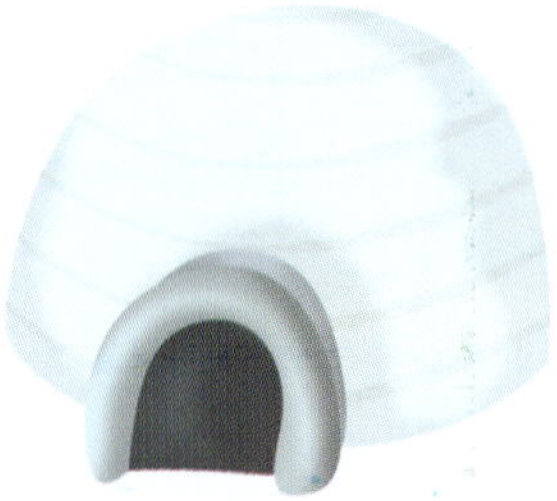

کلبه اسکیموها
kolbe'e eskimo ha

inch

inch اینچ

injection

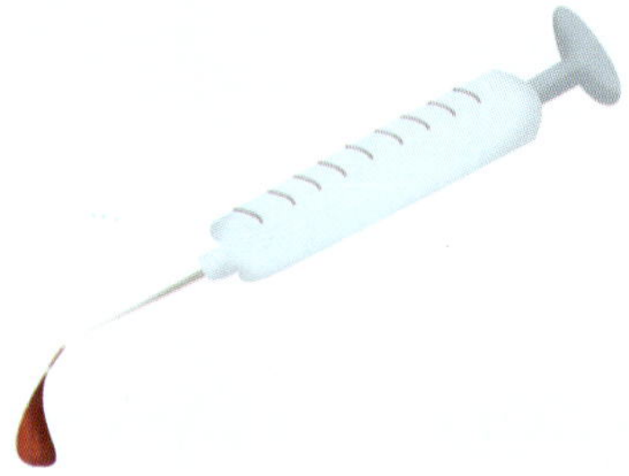

tazrig تزریق

injury

sadame صدمه

ink

johar جوهر

inn

مسافرخانه
mosaferkhane

insect

hashare حشره

inspector

bazras بازرس

instrument

saz ساز

internet

internet اینترنت

intestine
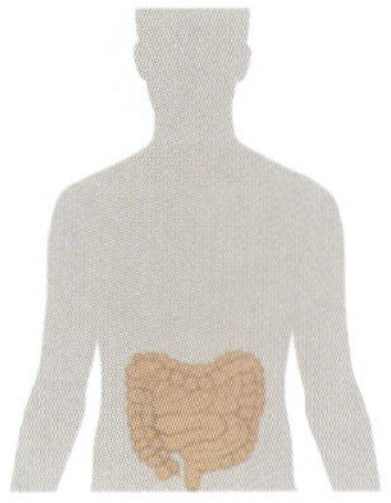

roode روده

inventor

mokhtare مخترع

invitation
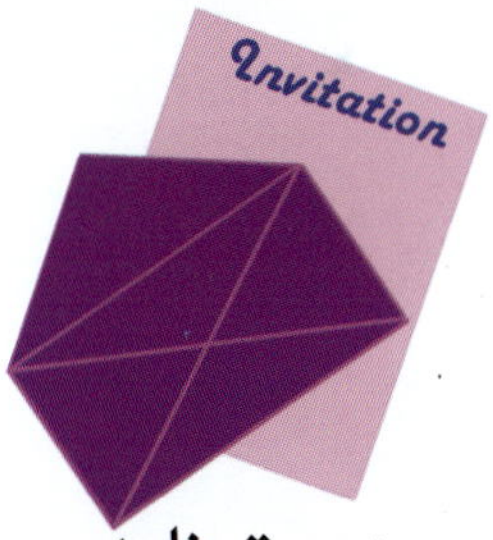

دعوت نامه
davatname

iron

otoo اتو

island

jazire جزیره

ivory

aaj عاج

a b c d e f g h i j k l m n o p q r s t u v w x y z

Jj

jackal

shoghal شغال

jacket

jakat ژاکت

jackfruit

جک فروت
jack froot

jam

morabba مربا

jar

shishe شیشه

javelin

پرتاب نیزه
partabe neyze

jaw

fak فک

jeans

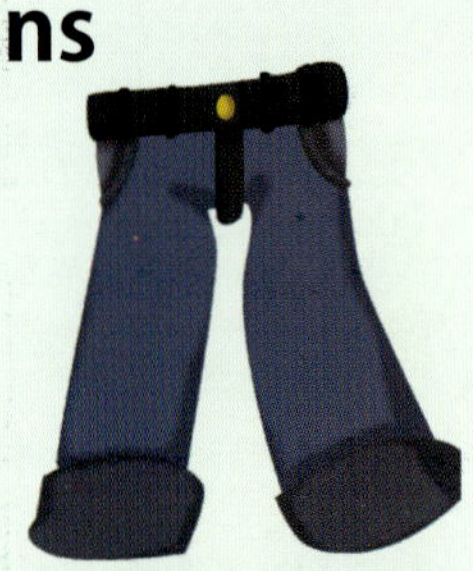

شلوار جین
shalvare jin

jelly

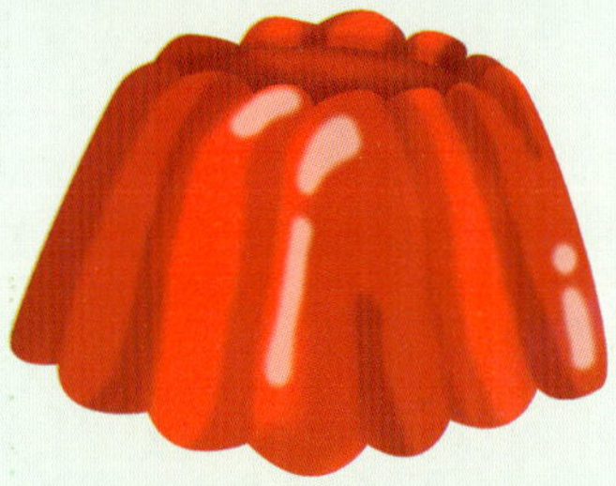

jele ژله

jetty

اسکله بندر
eskele bandar

jewellery
US English **jewelry**

jevaherat جواهرات

jigsaw

pazel پازل

jockey

savarkar سوارکار

joker

bazale goo بذله گو

journey

safar سفر

jug

kooze کوزه

juggler

شعبده باز
shobadeh baz

juice

ab mive آب میوه

jungle

jangal جنگل

jute

joot جوت

Kk

kangaroo

kangoro کانگورو

kennel

lane sag لانه سگ

kerb
US English **curb**

محدود کردن
mahdodkardan

kerosene

نفت سفید
nafte sefid

ketchup

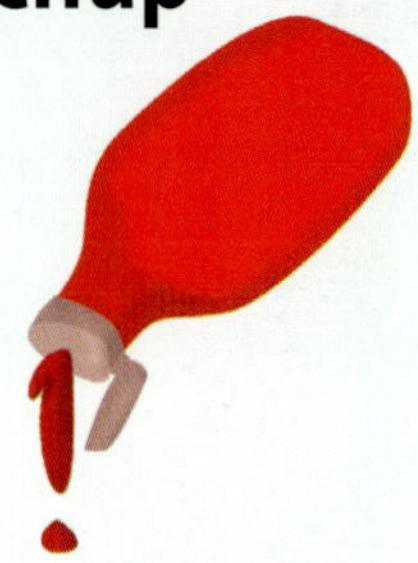

سس گوجه
sose goje

kettle

ketry کتری

key

kleed کلید

keyboard

صفحه کلید
safhe kleed

key ring

دسته کلید
daste kleed

kidney

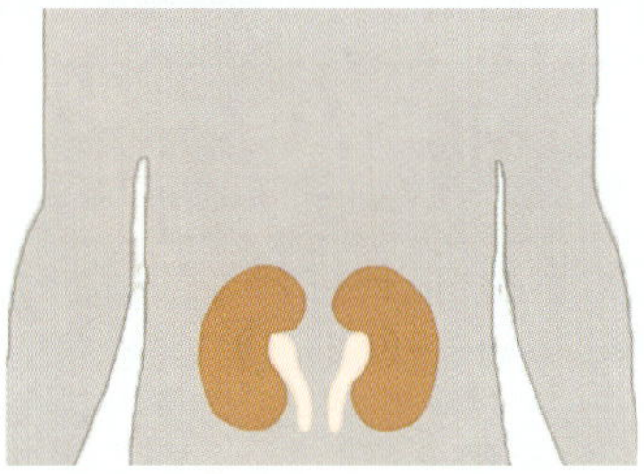

kollie کلیه

kilogram

kiloogram کیلوگرم

king

padeshah پادشاه

kiosk

dakke دکه

kiss

boose بوسه

kitchen

اشپزخانه
ashpazkhane

kite

badbadak بادبادک

kitten

بچه گربه
bache gorbe

kiwi

kivi کیوی

knee

zanoo زانو

knife

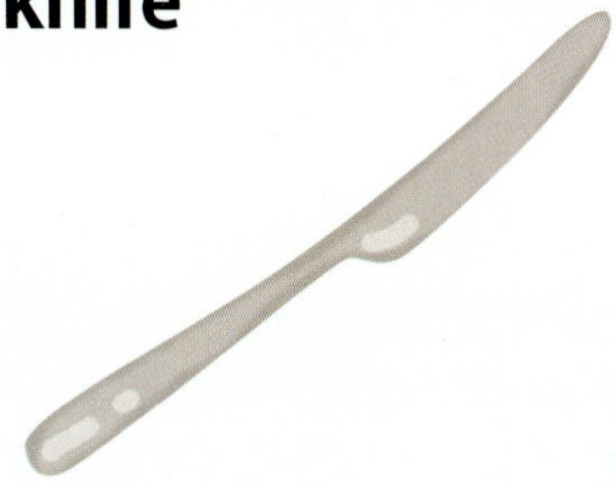

chaghoo چاقو

knight

shovalie شواليه

knitwear

لباس بافتنی
lebas baftany

knob

dastgire دستگیره

knock

dar zadan در زدن

knot

gereh گره

knuckle

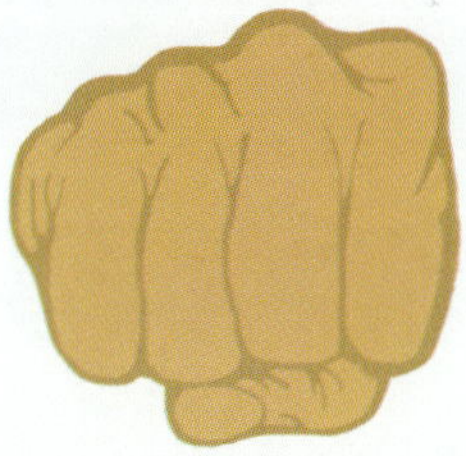

mosht مشت

Ll

label

barchasb برچسب

laboratory
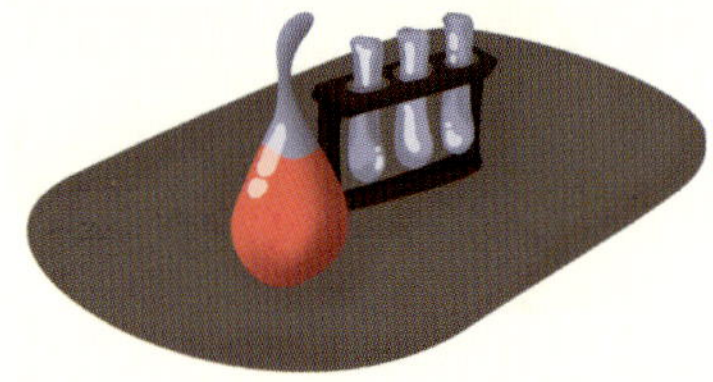

آزمایشگاه
azamayshgah

lace

بند کفش
bande kafsh

ladder

nardebaan نردبان

lady

khanoom خانم

ladybird
US English **ladybug**

کفش دوزک
kafsh doozak

lagoon

taalab تالاب

lake

daryache دریاچه

lamb

barre بره

lamp

laamp لامپ

lamp post
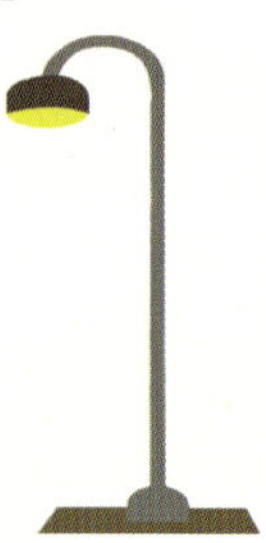

cheragh چراغ

land

zamin زمین

lane

masir مسیر

lantern

fanoos فانوس

laser

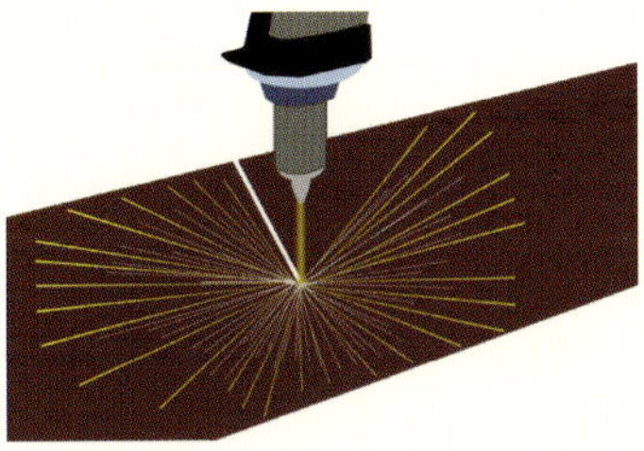

laser لیزر

lasso

kamand کمند

latch

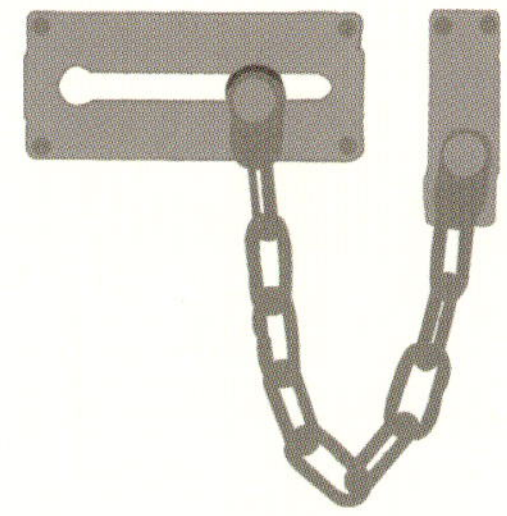

cheft چفت

laundry

خشکشویی
khosh shoee

lawn

chaman چمن

lawyer

vakil وکیل

layer

laye لایه

leaf

barg برگ

leather

charm چرم

leg

pa پا

lemon

limoo لیمو

lemonade

limonad لیموناد

lens

adasy عدسی

leopard

palang پلنگ

letter

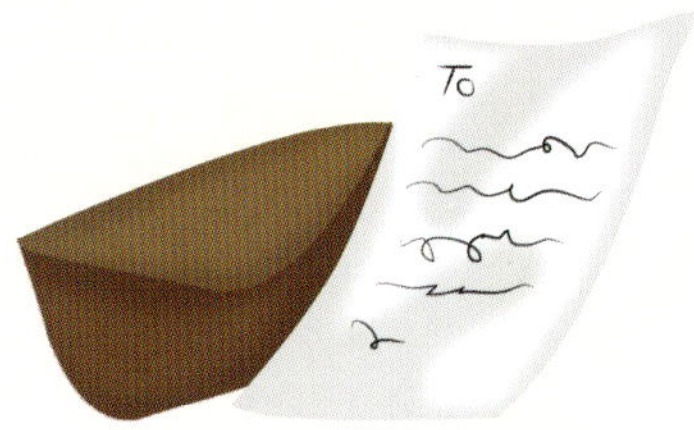

nam'e نامه

letterbox
US English **mailbox**

صندوق نامه
sandooge nam'e

lettuce

kahoo کاهو

library

ketabkhane کتابخانه

licence

mojavez مجوز

lid

dar در

light

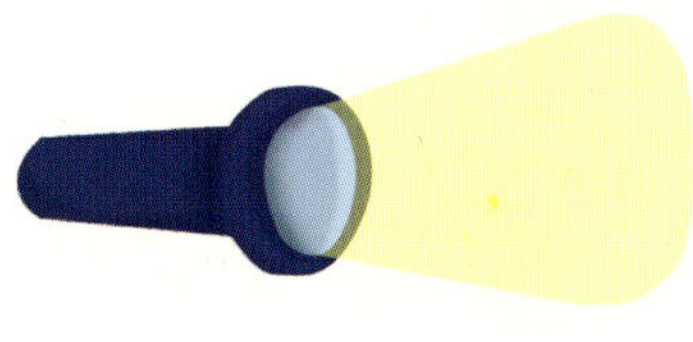

چراغ قوه
cheragh ghovve

lighthouse

فانوس دریایی
fanoos daryaee

limb

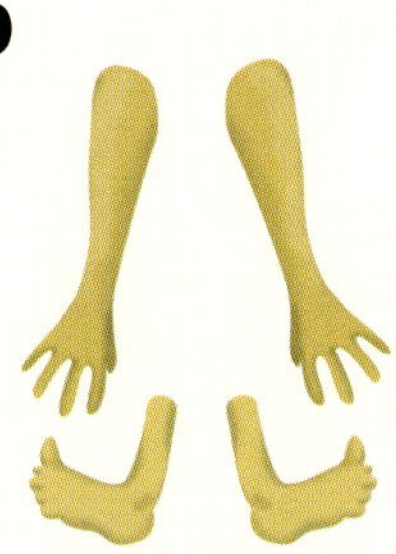

عضو بدن
ozve badan

line

khat خط

lion

shire nar شیر نر

lip

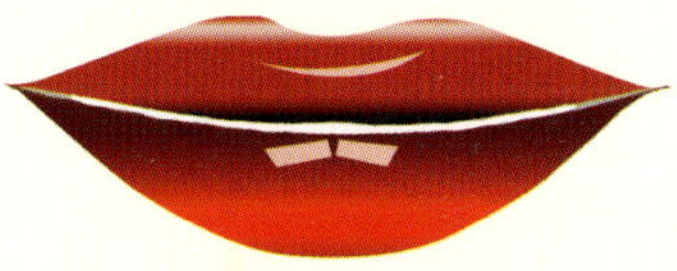

lab لب

lipstick

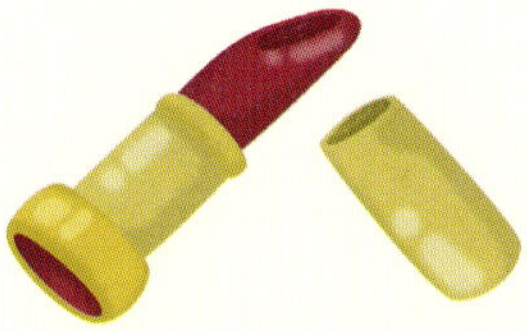

roje lab رژ لب

liquid

maye مایع

list

feyhrest فهرست

litre
US English **liter**

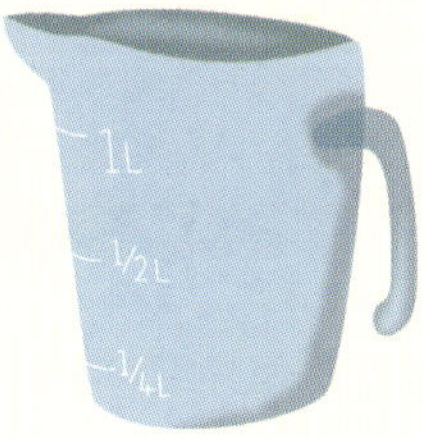

litr لیتر

living room

hall هال

lizard

marmoolak مارمولک

load

bar بار

loaf

ghorse naan قرص نان

lobster

خرچنگ دریایی
kharchange daryaee

lock

ghofl قفل

loft

saghf سقف

log

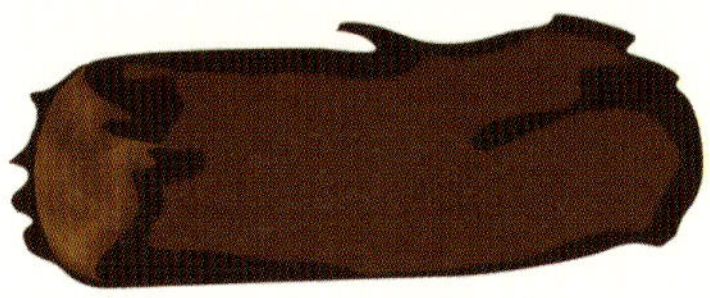

تکه چوب
tekke choob

loop

halghe حلقه

lorry
US English **truck**

kamion کامیون

lotus

gol گل

louse

shepesh شپش

luggage

chamedan چمدان

lunch

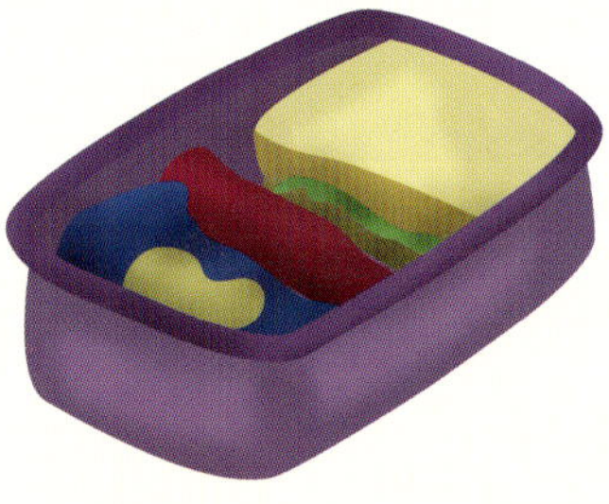

nahar ناهار

lung

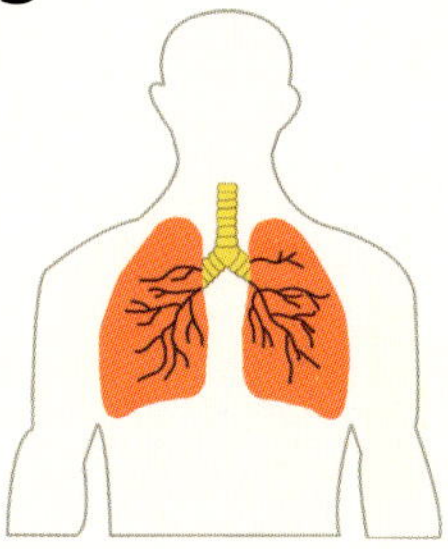

reeyeh ریه

Mm

machine

dastgah دستگاه

magazine

majalle مجله

magician

شعبده باز
shobade baz

magnet

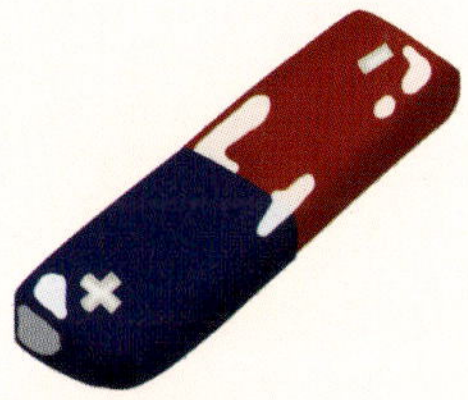

ahanroba آهن ربا

magpie

zaaghy زاغی

mail

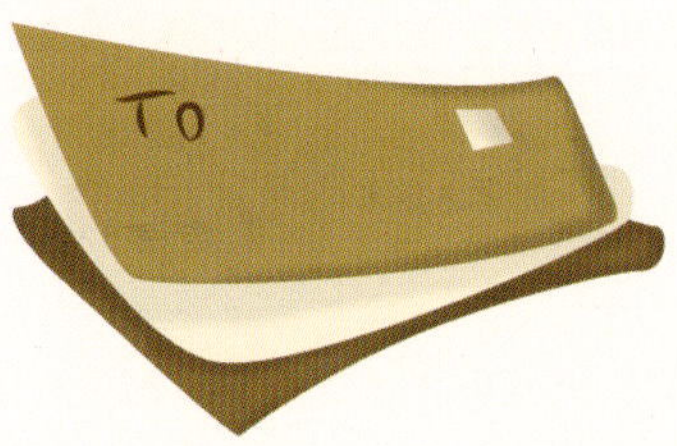

post پست

mammal

پستاندار
pestandar

man

mard مرد

mandolin

mandolin ماندولین

mango

anbe انبه

map

nagshe نقشه

a b c d e f g h i j k l **m** n o p q r s t u v w x y z

a b c d e f g h i j k l m n o p q r s t u v w x y z

maple

afra افرا

marble

سنگ مرمر
sange marmar

market

bazaar بازار

mask

maask ماسک

mast

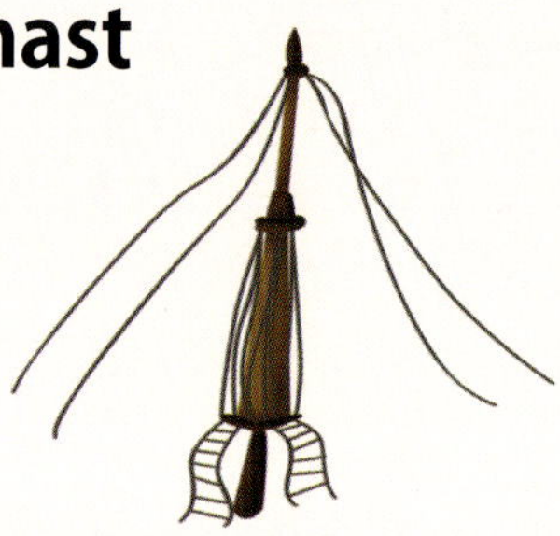

tir تیر

mat

hasir حصیر

matchbox

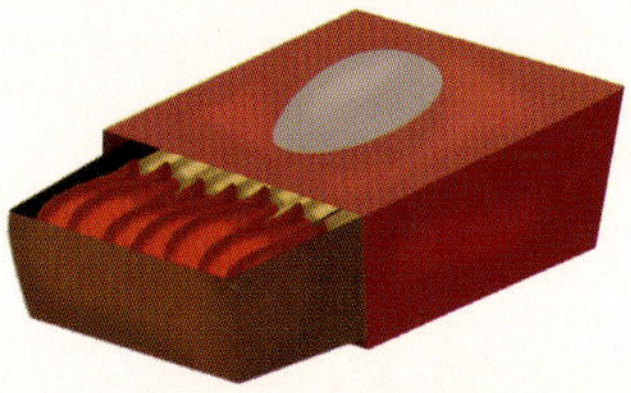

قوطی کبریت
ghoty kebrit

mattress

toshak تشک

meal

وعده غذایی
vade ghazaee

meat

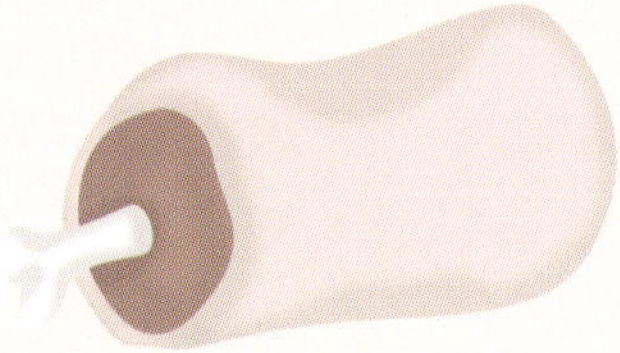

goosht گوشت

mechanic

mekanik مکانیک

medicine

daroo دارو

melon

kharbozeh خربوزه

merchant

tajer تاجر

mermaid

پری دریایی
parye daryaee

metal

falez فلز

metre

US English **meter**

metr متر

microphone

میکروفن
mikrofon

microwave

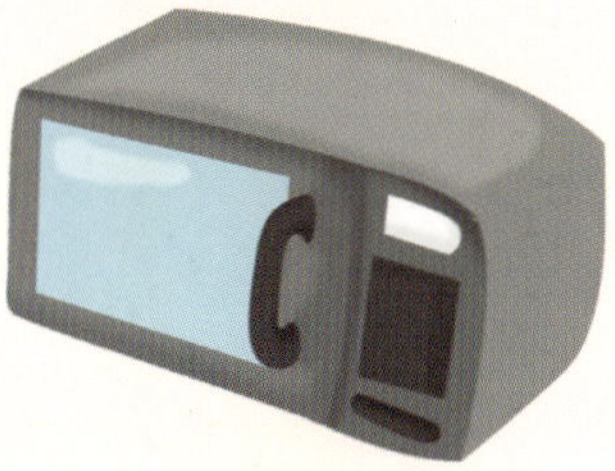

مایکروویو
microwave

mile

mile مایل

milk

shir شیر

miner

madan chi معدن چی

mineral

madany معدنی

mint

na'ana نعناع

minute

daghighe دقیقه

mirror

ayne آینه

mobile phone

تلفن همراه
telfone hamrah

model

model مدل

mole

khal خال

money

pool پول

monk

raheb راهب

monkey

meymoon میمون

monster

hayoola هیولا

month

mah ماه

monument

بنای تاریخی
banaye tarikhee

moon

mah ماه

mop

پاک کردن
pak kardan

morning

sobh صبح

mosquito

pashe پشه

moth

بید پروانه
bide parvane

mother

madar مادر

motorcycle

موتورسیکلت
motorsiklet

motorway

bozorgrah بزرگراه

mountain

kooh کوه

mouse

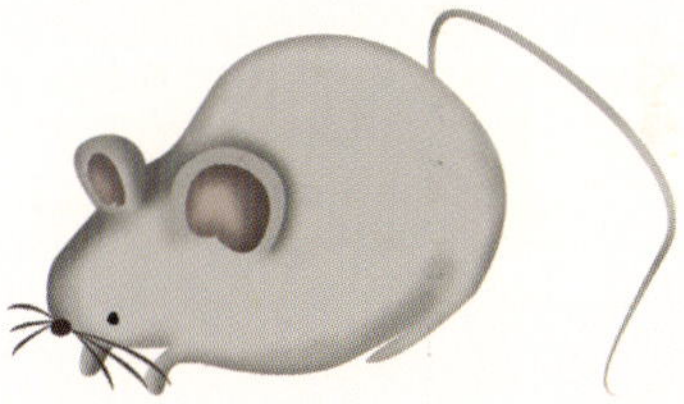

moosh موش

mousetrap

tal'e mush تله موش

moustache

sibil سبیل

mouth

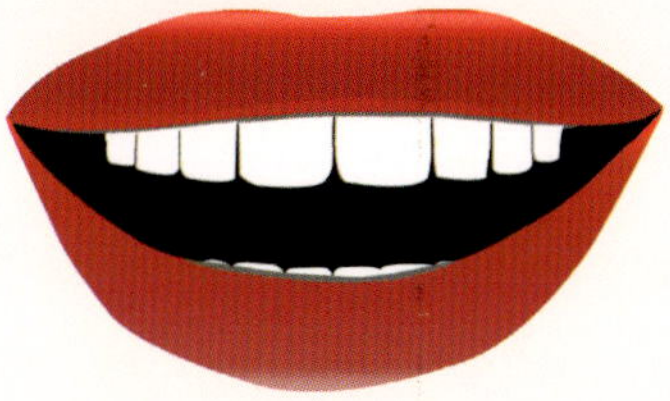

dahan دهان

a b c d e f g h i j k l m n o p q r s t u v w x y z

mud

gel o lay گل و لای

muffin

بشقاب سفالی کوچک
boshgabe sofalie koochak

mug

livan لیوان

mule

ghater قاطر

muscle

azole عضله

museum

mooze موزه

mushroom

قارچ خوراکی
qarch khorki

music

moosighi موسیقی

musician

navazande نوازنده

Nn

nail

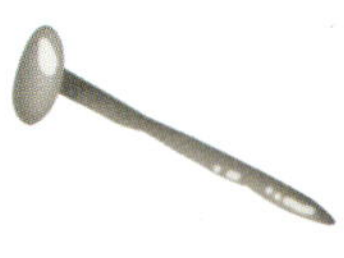

mikh میخ

napkin

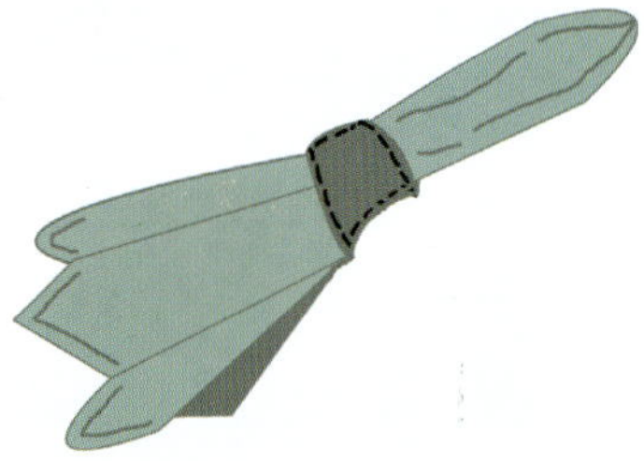

dastmal دستمال

nappy
US English **diaper**

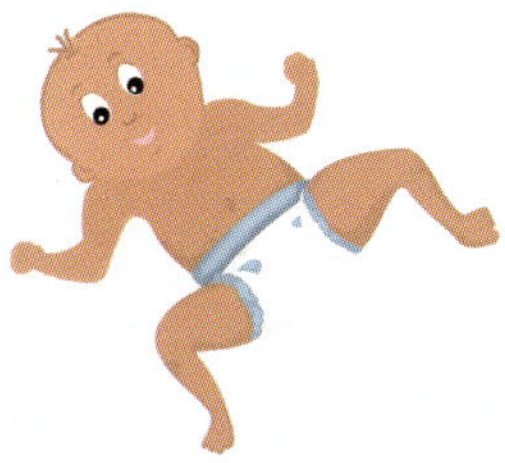

pooshak پوشک

nature

tabeeat طبیعت

neck

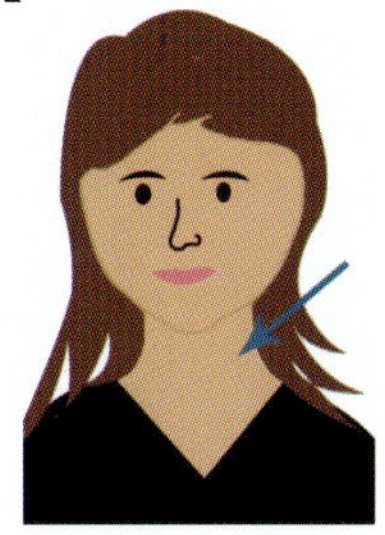

gardan گردن

necklace

گردن بند
gardanband

necktie

karavat کراوات

needle

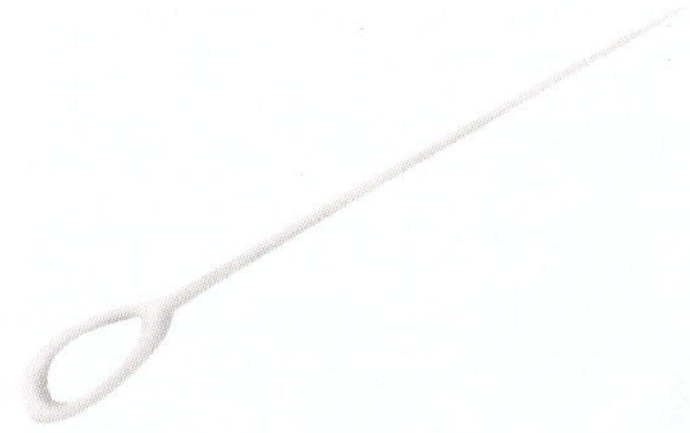

soozan سوزن

neighbour
US English **neighbor**

hamsaye همسایه

nest

lane لانه

net

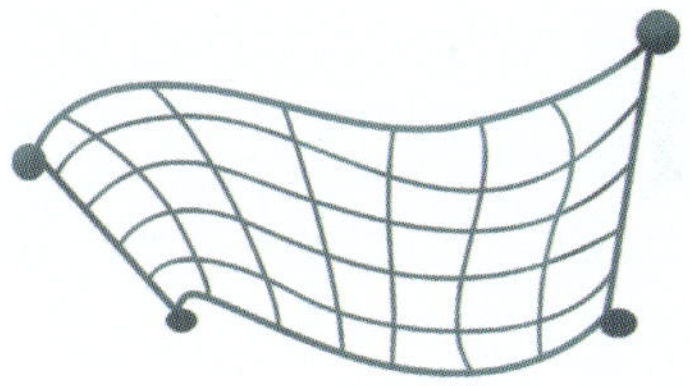

toori توری

newspaper

rozname روزنامه

night

shab شب

nine

noh نه

noodles

noodle نودل

noon

zohr ظهر

north

shomal شمال

nose

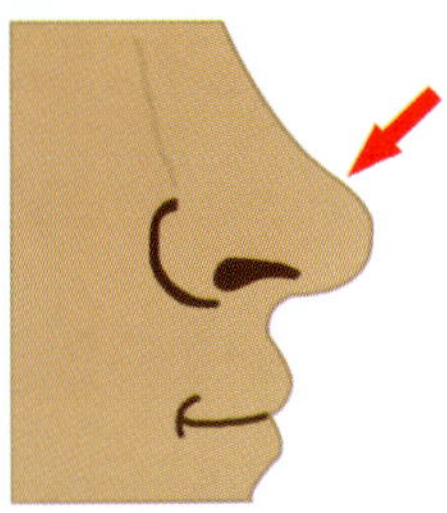

binee بینی

note

nokte نکته

notebook

دفتر یادداشت
daftar yaddasht

notice

ittela اطلاع

number

adad عدد

nun

rahebe راهبه

nurse

parastar پرستار

nursery

golkhane گلخانه

nut

ajeel آجیل

Oo

oar

paroo پارو

observatory

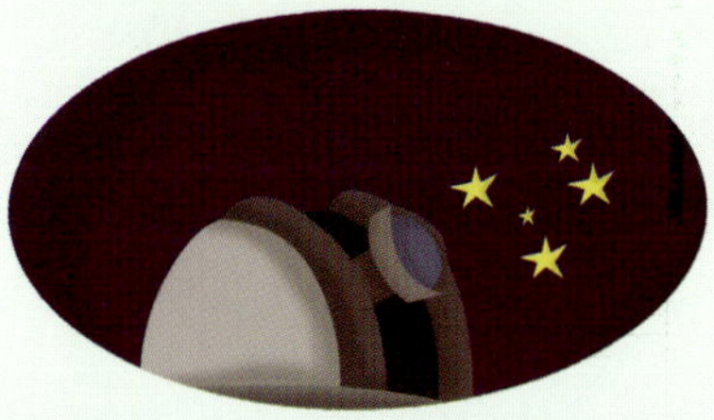

رصد خانه
rasadkhane

ocean

oghyanoos اقیانوس

octopus

hashtpa هشت پا

office

daftar دفتر

oil

naft نفت

olive

zaytoon زیتون

omelette

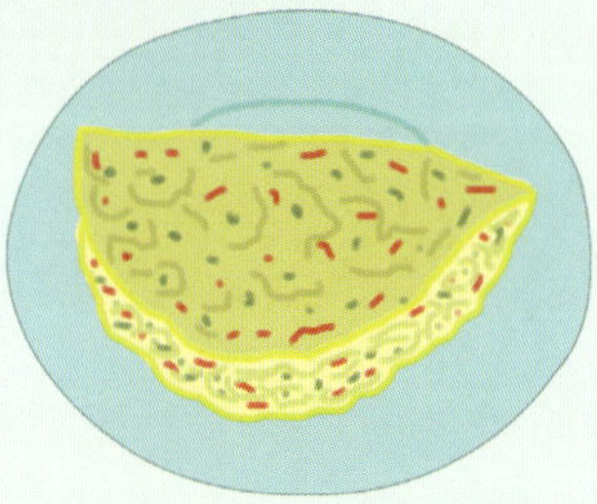

omlet املت

one

yek یک

onion

peeaz پیاز

orange

narenjee نارنجی

a b c d e f g h i j k l m n o p q r s t u v w x y z

orbit

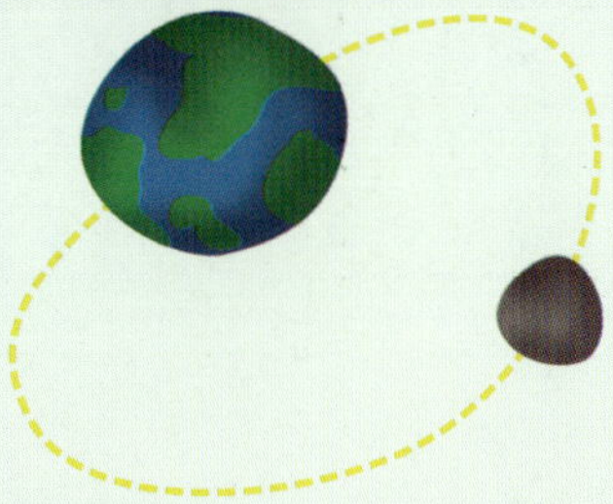

madar مدار

orchard

bagestan باغستان

orchestra

orkestr ارکستر

ostrich

شتر مرغ
shotrmorg

otter

سمور دریایی
samore daryaee

oval

beyzee بیضی

oven

fer فر

owl

joghd جغد

ox

gaave nar گاو نر

Pp

packet

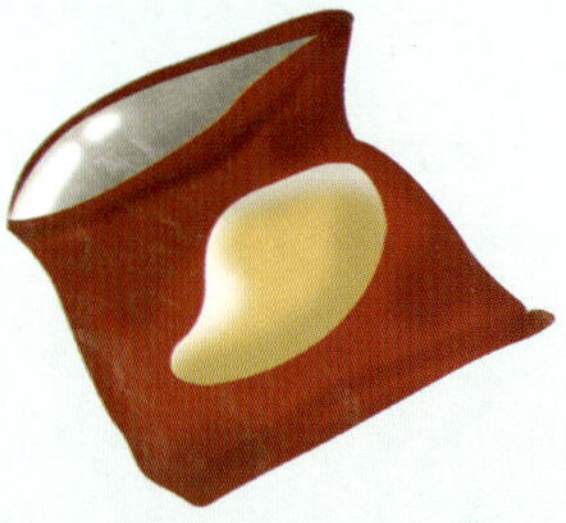

baste بسته

page

safhe صفحه

pain

dard درد

paint

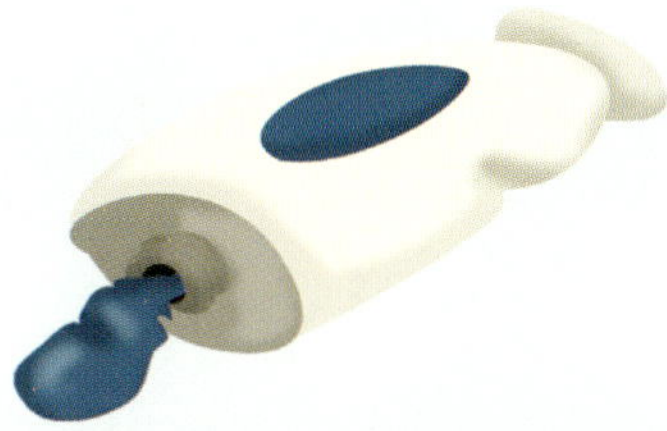

rang رنگ

painting

رنگ آمیزی
rangameezee

pair

joft جفت

palace

ghasr قصر

palm

kafe dast کف دست

pan

maytabe ماهی تابه

pancake

pancake پن کیک

panda

panda پاندا

papaya

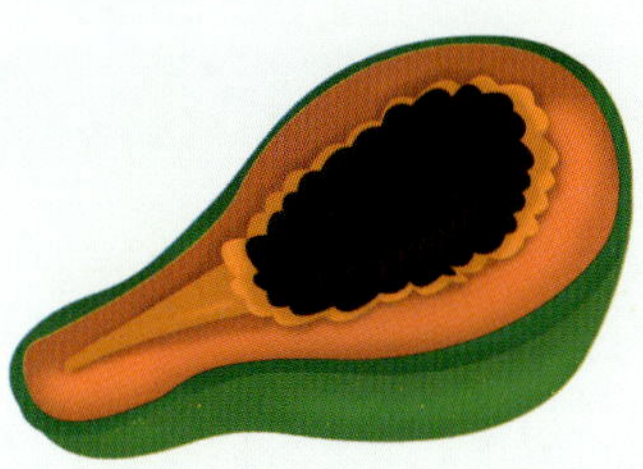

papaya پاپایا

paper

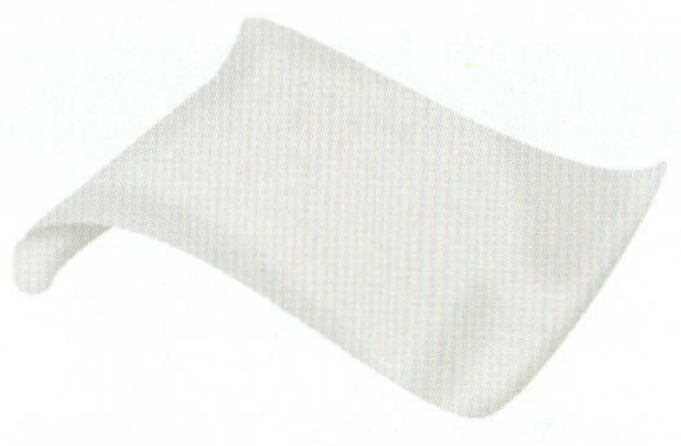

kagaz کاغذ

parachute

چتر نجات
chatare nejat

parcel

baste بسته

park

park پارک

parrot

tooty طوطی

passenger

mosafer مسافر

pasta

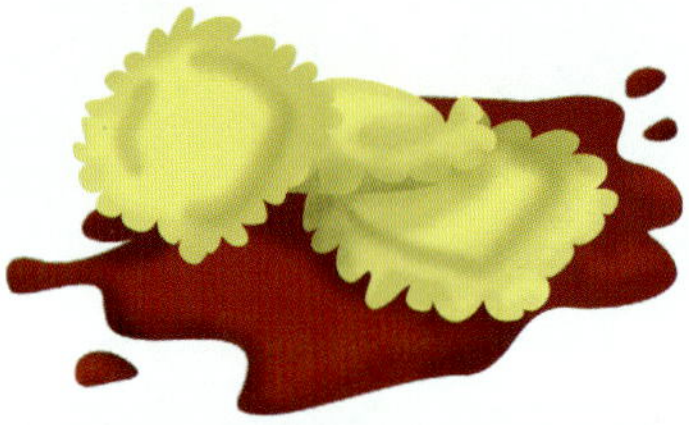

pasta پاستا

pastry

shireenee شیرینی

pavement

peadero پیاده رو

paw

panje پنجه

pea

nokhod نخود

peach

holoo هلو

peacock

tavvoos طاووس

peak

oaj اوج

peanut

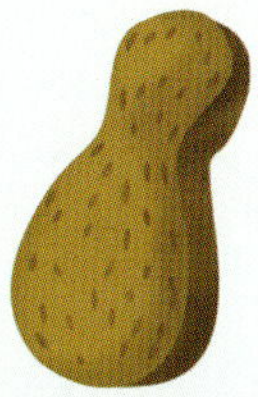

بادام زمینی

badam zaminee

pear

golabi گلابی

pearl

morvarid مروارید

pedal

padal پدال

pelican

مرغ ماهیخوار

morghe mahikhar

pen

khodkar خودکار

pencil

medad مداد

penguin

pangooan پنگوین

pepper

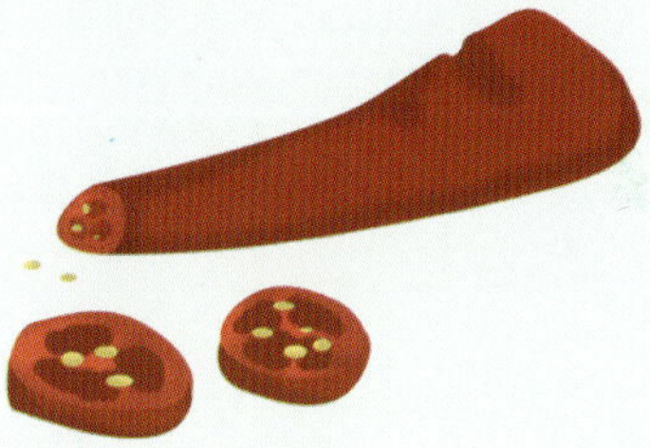

felfel فلفل

perfume

atr عطر

pet

حیوان خانگی

heyvane khanegy

pharmacy

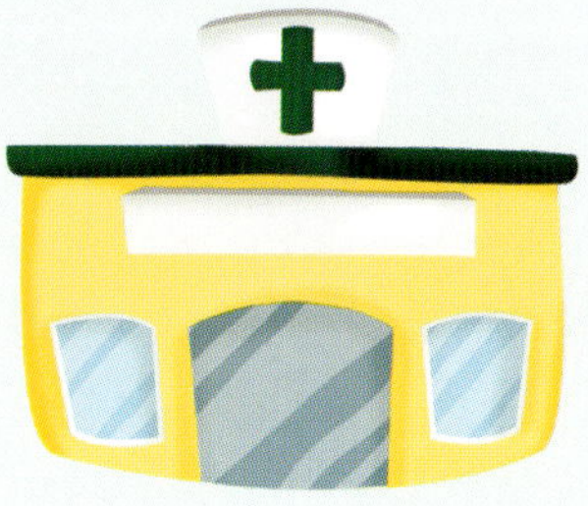

darookane داروخانه

photograph

aks عکس

piano

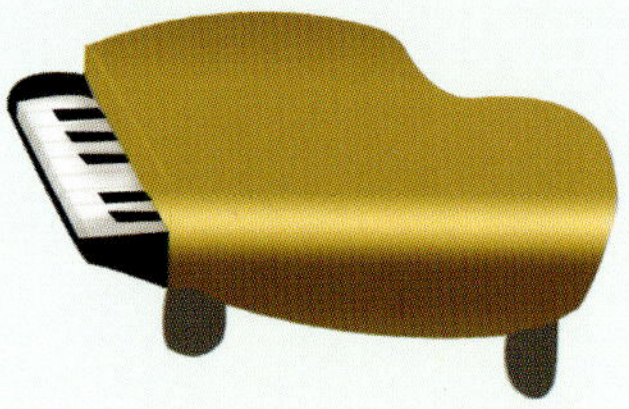

piano پیانو

picture

tasvir تصویر

pie

pie پای

pig

khook خوک

pigeon

kabootar کبوتر

pillar

sotoon ستون

pillow

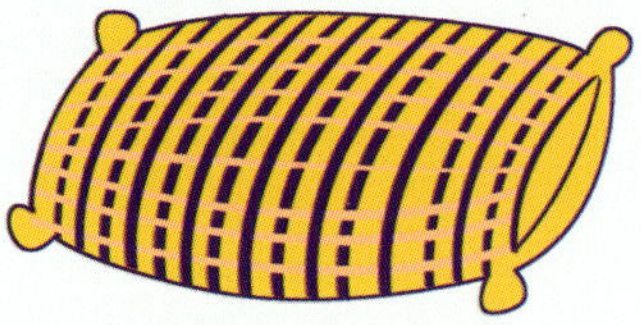

balesh بالش

pilot

khalaban خلبان

pineapple

ananas آناناس

pink

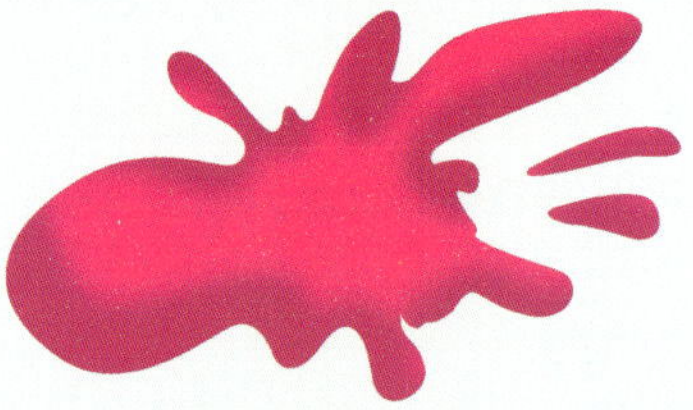

رنگ صورتی
range sooratee

pipe

loole لوله

pizza

pitza پیتزا

planet

sayare سیاره

plant

geeaah گیاه

plate

boshgab بشقاب

platform

sakkoo سکو

platypus

platypus پلاتیپوس

player

bazicon بازیکن

plum

aloo آلو

plumber

lolekesh لوله کش

plywood

تخته چندلا
takhte chandla

pocket

jeab جیب

poet

sha'er شاعر

polar bear

خرس قطبی
kherse ghotbee

police

police پلیس

pollution

aloodegy الودگی

pomegranate

anar انار

pond

hozche حوضچه

porcupine

جوجه تیغی
joje teeghee

port

bandar بندر

porter

baarbar باربر

postcard

کارت پستال
carte postal

postman

postcheee پستچی

post office

اداره پست
dare'e post

pot

goldan گلدان

potato

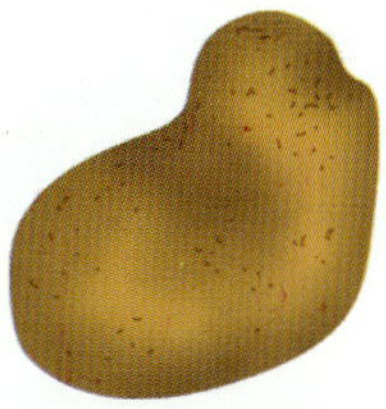

سیب زمینی
sib zaminee

powder

poodr پودر

prawn
US English **shrimp**

meygoo میگو

priest

mujtahid مجتهد

prince

shahzade شاهزاده

prison

zendan زندان

pudding

pooding پودینگ

pump

tolombe تلمبه

pumpkin

كدو حلوايي
kado halvae

puppet

aroosak عروسک

puppy

toole sag توله سگ

purse

کیف زنانه
kif zanaane

Qq

quail

belderchin بلدرچین

quarry

معدن سنگ
madane sang

queen

malake ملکه

queue

saf صف

quiver

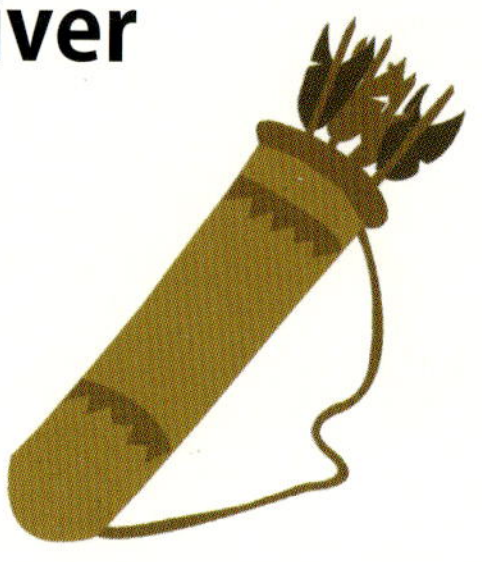

tirdan تیردان

Rr

rabbit

khargoosh خرگوش

rack

ghafase قفسه

racket

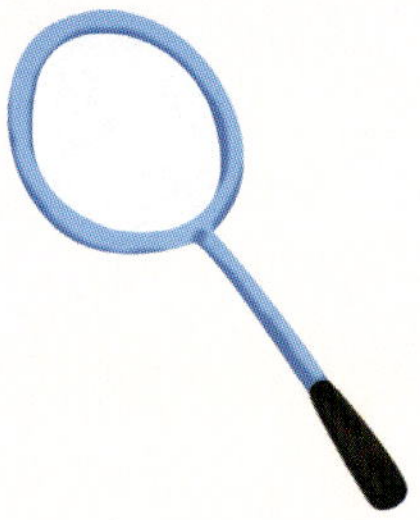

راکت تنیس
raket tenis

radio

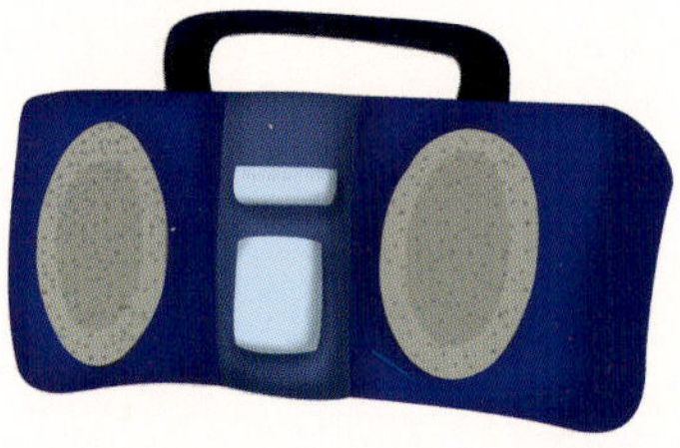

radio رادیو

radish

torobche تربچه

raft

ghayegh قایق

rain

baaran باران

rainbow

رنگین کمان
rangin kaman

raisin

keshmesh کشمش

ramp

سطح شیب دار
sathe shibdar

raspberry

tameshk تمشک

rat

moosh موش

razor

تیغ صورت تراشی
tige soorat tarashy

receipt

resid رسید

rectangle

مربع مستطیل
morab'a mostateel

red

sorkh سرخ

restaurant

restooran رستوران

rhinoceros

kargadan کرگدن

rib

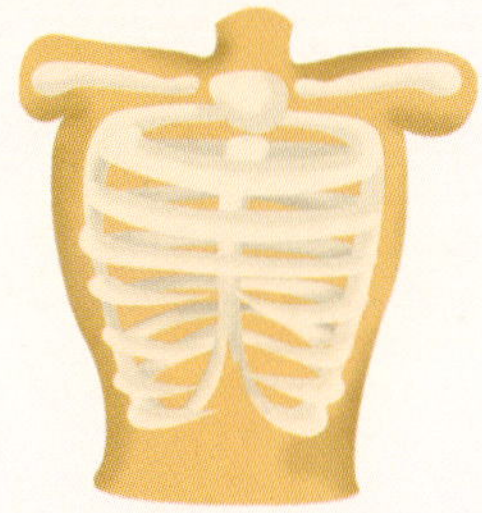

dande دنده

ribbon

rooban روبان

rice

berenj برنج

ring

halgheh حلقه

river

رودخانه/رود
rodkhaneh/rod

road

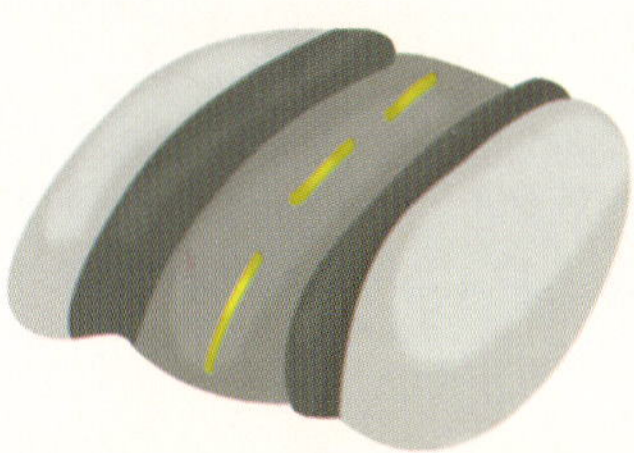

jadde جاده

robber

dozd دزد

robe

لباس بلند و گشاد
lebase boland va goshad

robot

robot ربات

rock

sang سنگ

rocket

mooshak موشک

roller coaster

ترن هوایی
teran havaee

room

otak اتاق

root

rishe ریشه

rope

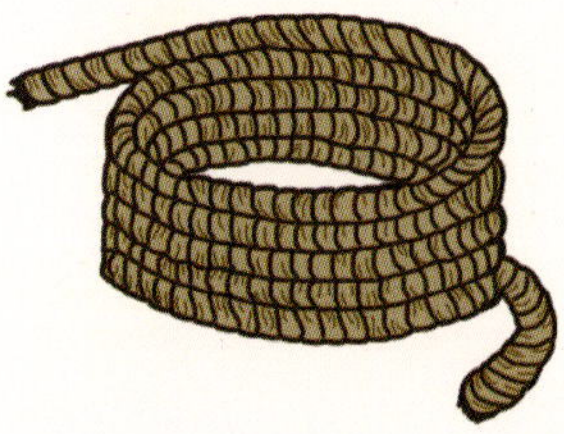

tanab طناب

rose

gole sorkh گل سرخ

round

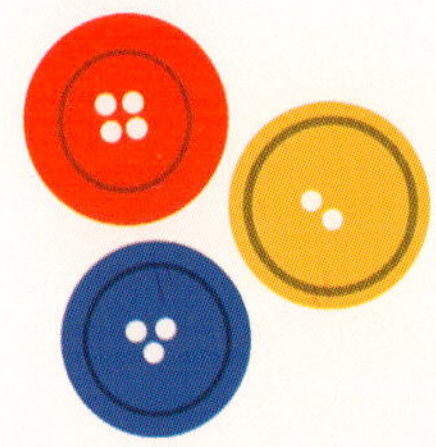

gerd گرد

rug

galeche قالیچه

rugby

ragbee راگبی

ruler

khatkesh خط کش

Ss

sack

keese کیسه

sail

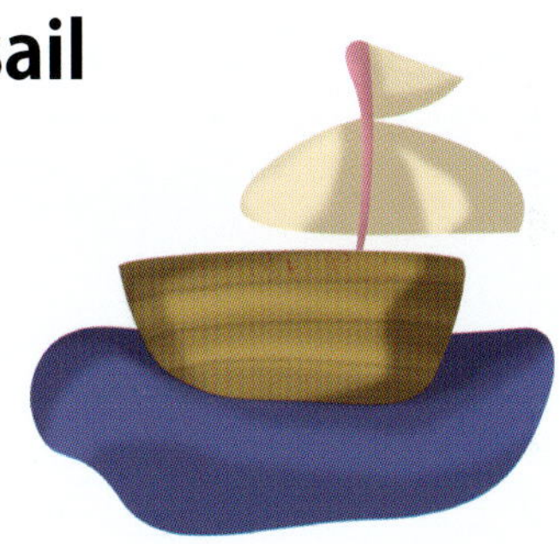

badban بادبان

a b c d e f g h i j k l m n o p q r s t u v w x y z

a b c d e f g h i j k l m n o p q r s t u v w x y z

sailor

malavan ملوان

salad

salad سالاد

salt

namak نمک

sand

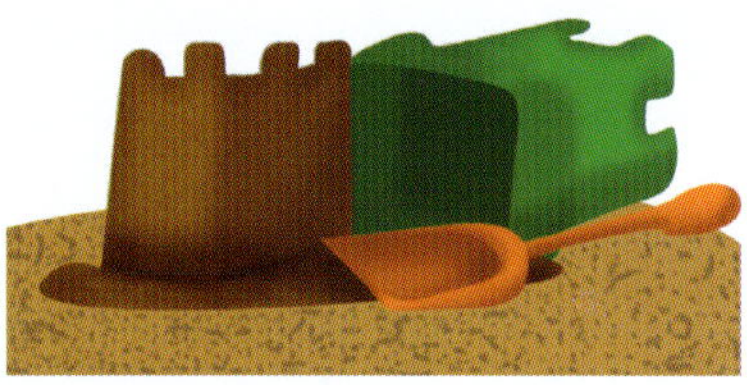

shen شن

sandwich

ساندویچ
sandevich

satellite

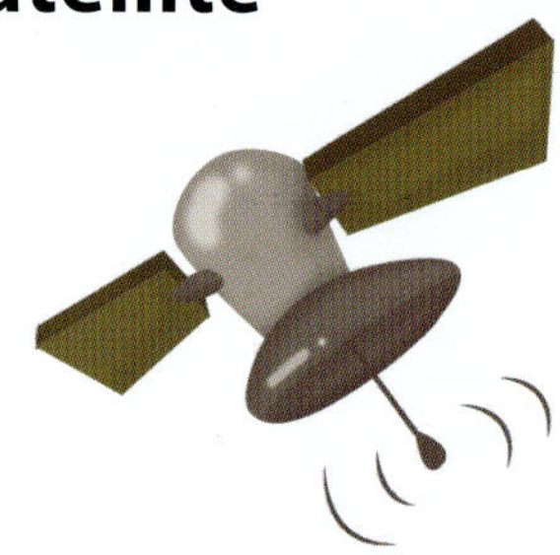

mahvare ماهواره

saucer

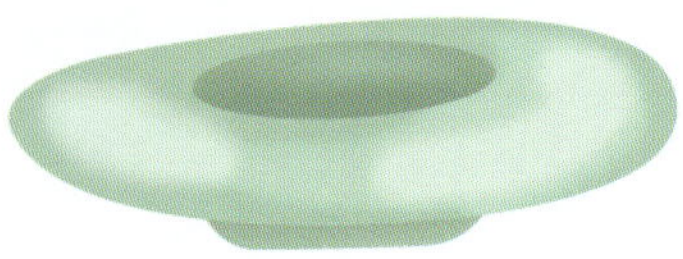

بشقاب کوچك /نعلبكي
boshgabe koochak / nalbaki

sausage

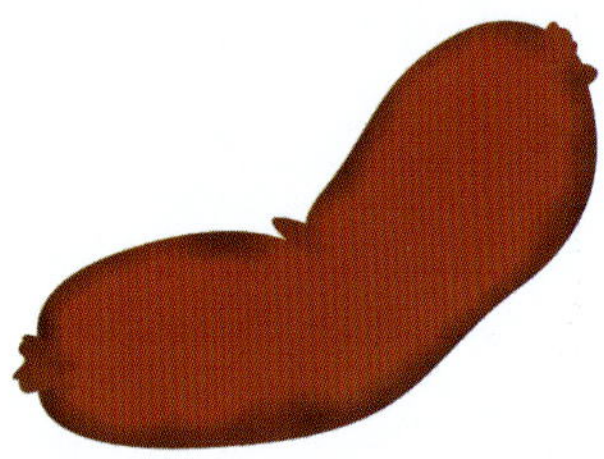

sosees سوسیس

saw

arre اره

scarf

shal شال

school

maktab مکتب

scissors

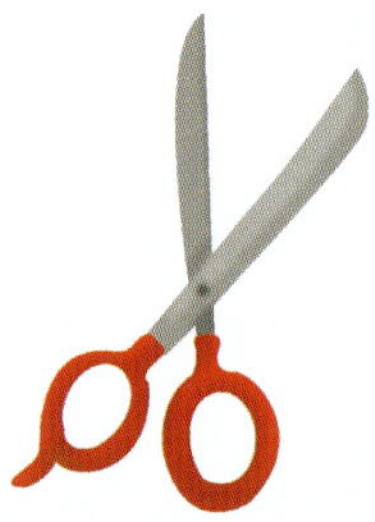

gheychee قیچی

scooter

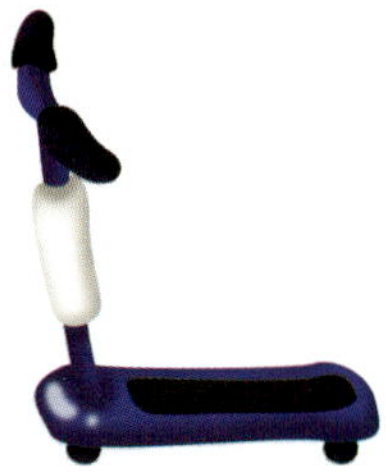

scooter اسکوتر

scorpion

aghrab عقرب

screw

peach پیچ

sea

darya دریا

seal

mohr مهر

seat

sandaly صندلی

see-saw

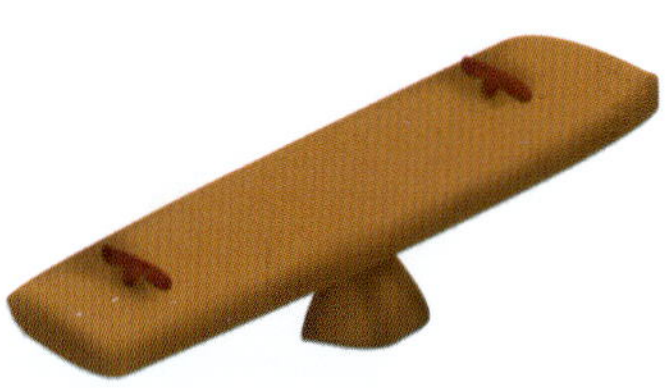

ala kolang الاکلنگ

seven

haft هفت

shadow

saye سایه

shampoo

shampoo شامپو

shark

koose کوسه

sheep

goosfand گوسفند

a b c d e f g h i j k l m n o p q r s t u v w x y z

shelf

taghche تاقچه

shell

pooste پوسته

shelter

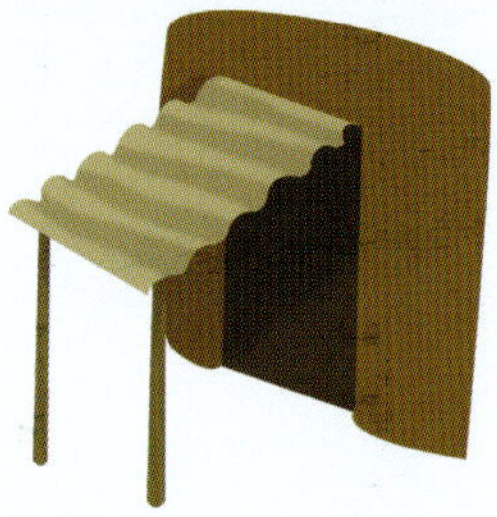

panah پناه

ship

keshty کشتی

shirt

pirahan پیراهن

shoe

kafsh کفش

shorts

شلوار کوتاه
shalvare kootah

shoulder

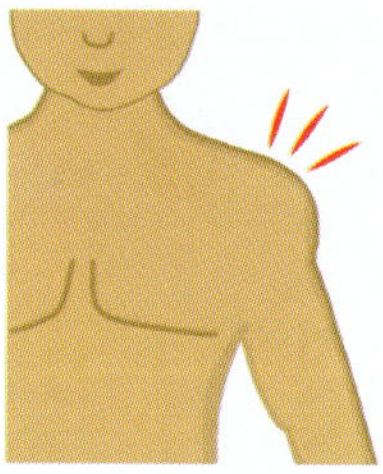

shane شانه

shower

doosh دوش

shutter

پشت پنجره
poshte panjere

shuttlecock

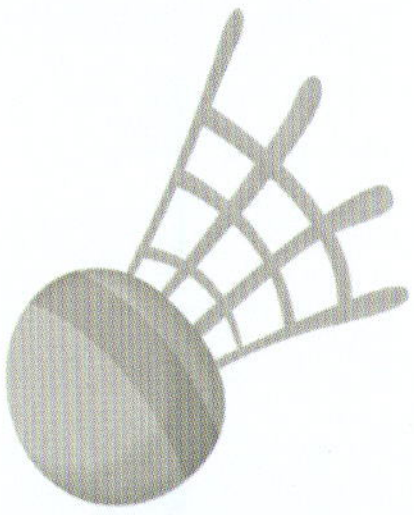

گوی پردار
goye pardar

signal

signal سیگنال

silver

noghre نقره

sink

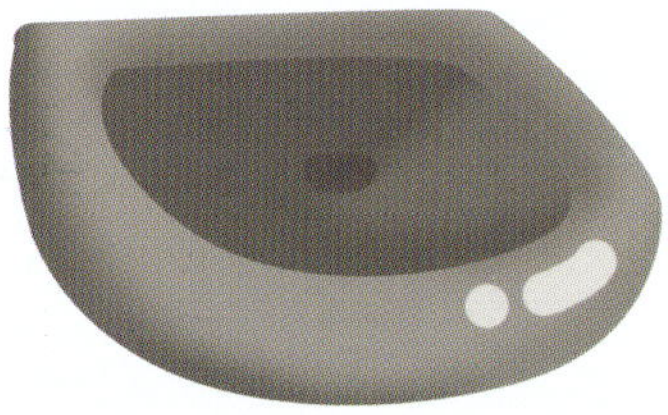

sink سینک

sister

khahar خواهر

six

shesh شش

skate

eskeyt اسکیت

skeleton

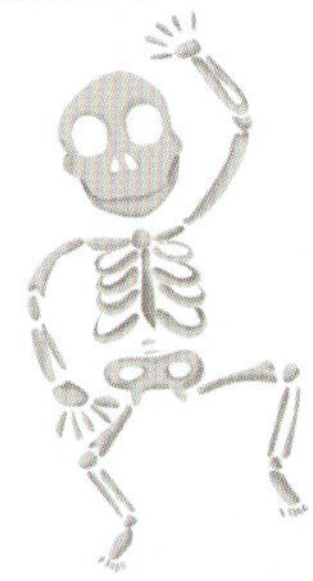

eskelet اسکلت

ski

eski اسکی

skin

poost پوست

skirt

daman دامن

skull

jomjome جمجمه

sky

aseman آسمان

skyscraper

آسمان خراش
asemankharash

slide

laghzesh لغزش

slipper

کفش راحتی/دمپايي
kafshe rahaty/ dampaee

smoke

dood دود

snail

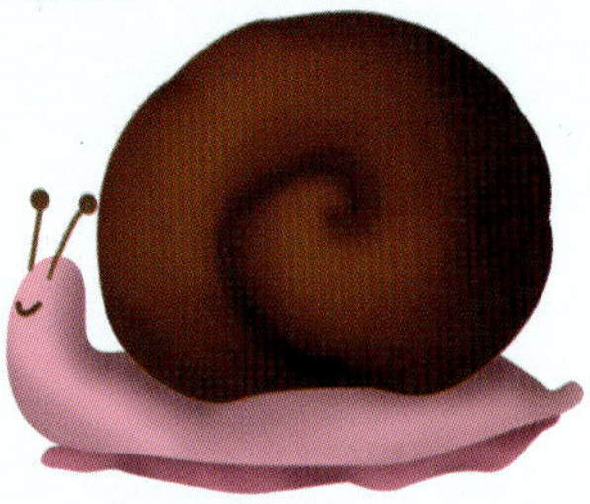

halazoon حلزون

snake

mar مار

snow

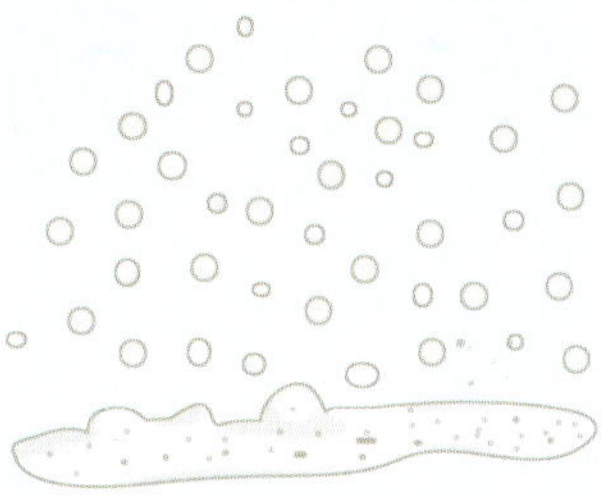

barf برف

soap

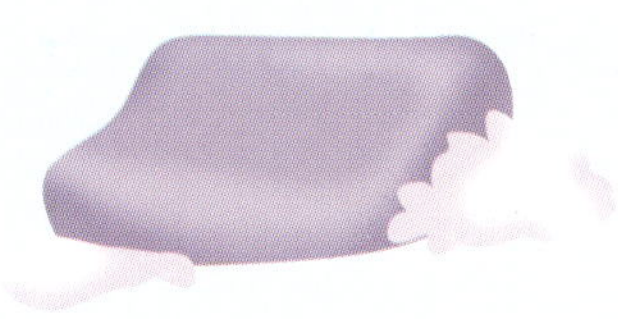

saboon صابون

sock

joorab جوراب

sofa

kanape کاناپه

soil

khak خاک

soldier

sarbaz سرباز

soup

soop سوپ

space

faza فضا

spaghetti

espagety اسپاگتی

sphere
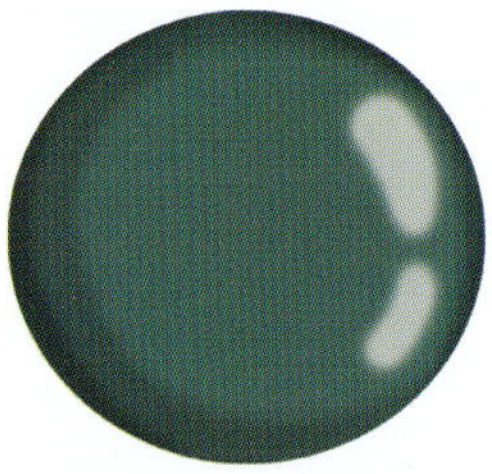

kore کره

spider

ankaboot عنکبوت

spinach

esfenaj اسفناج

sponge

esfanj اسفنج

spoon

ghashogh قاشق

spray

espray اسپری

spring

bahar بهار

square

marabaa مربع

squirrel

sanjab سنجاب

stadium

varzeshgah ورزشگاه

stairs

pelle ha پله ها

stamp

mohr مهر

star

setare ستاره

station

eestgah ایستگاه

statue

مجسمه
mojassame

stethoscope

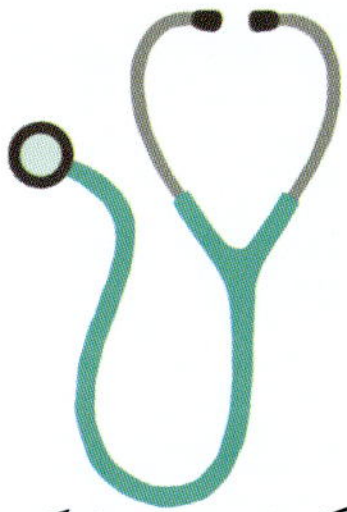

گوشی پزشکی
goosheye pezeshky

stomach

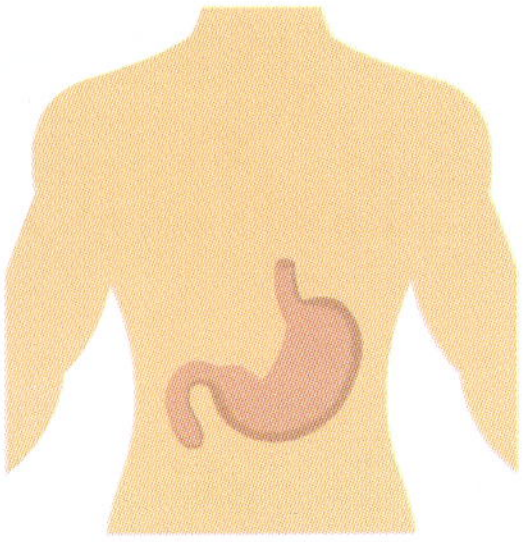

mede معده

stone

sang سنگ

storm

toofan طوفان

straw

nay نی

strawberry

توت فرنگی
toot farangy

street

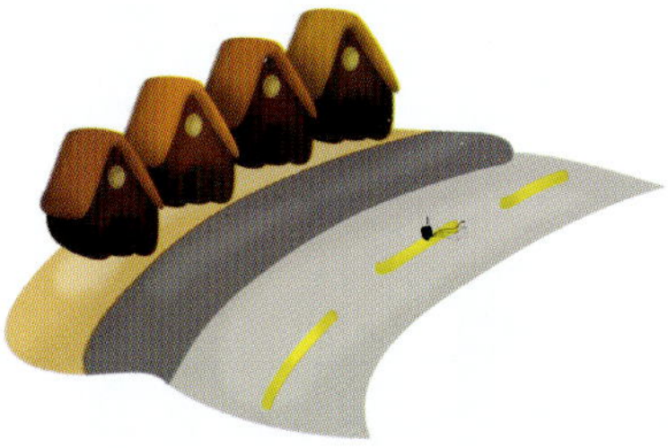

khyaban خیابان

student

daneshjoo دانشجو

submarine

زیر دریایی
zirdaryaee

subway

metro مترو

sugar

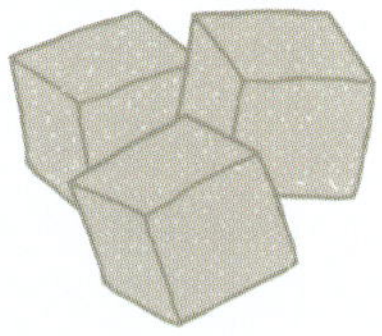

ghand قند

sugarcane

neyshekar نیشکر

summer

tabestan تابستان

sun

aftab آفتاب

supermarket

سوپر مارکت
supermarket

swan

ghoo قو

sweet

shireen شیرین

swimming pool

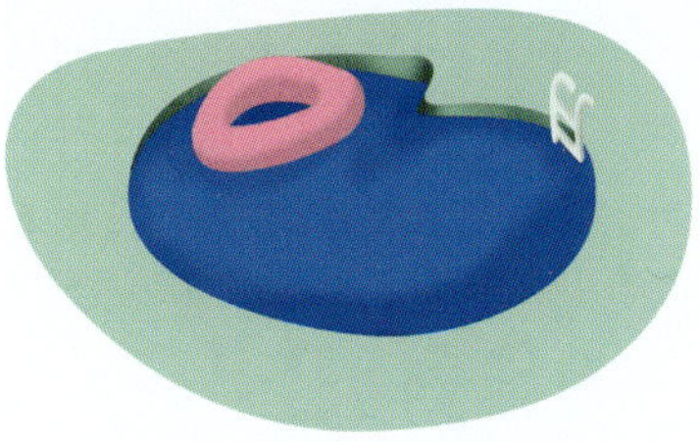

estakhr استخر

swimsuit

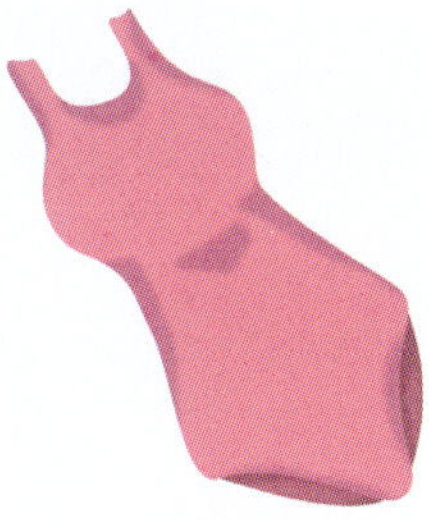

لباس شنا
lebase shena

a b c d e f g h i j k l m n o p q r s t u v w x y z

swing

تاب خوردن
tab khordan

switch

keleed کلید

syrup

sharbat شربت

Tt

table

jadval جدول

tall

gad boland قد بلند

tank

tank تانک

taxi

taxi تاکسی

tea

chai چای

teacher

moalem معلم

teeth

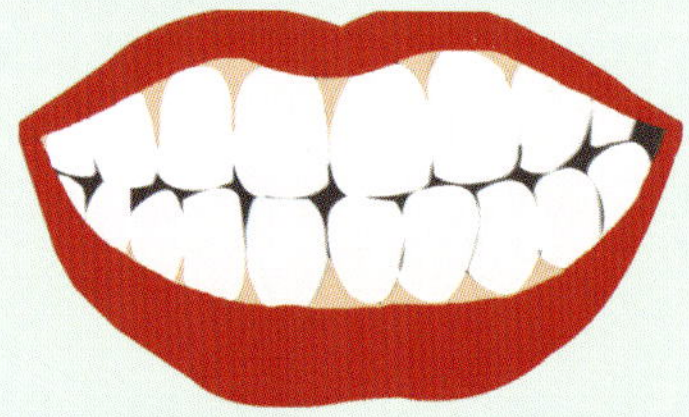

dandan ha دندانها

telephone

telefon تلفن

television

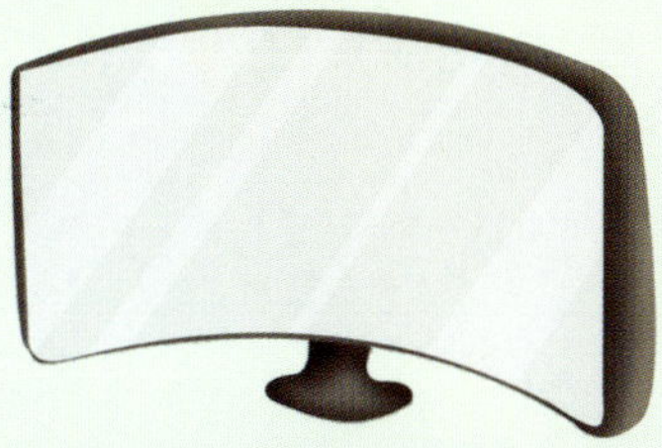

تلویزیون
televezeon

ten

dah ده

tennis

tennis تنیس

tent

chador چادر

thief

dozd دزد

thread

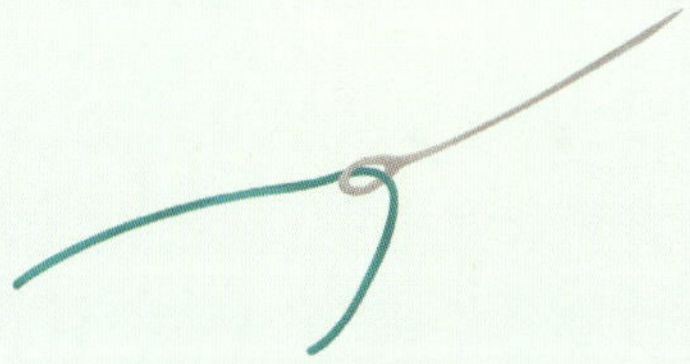

nakh نخ

three

se سه

throat

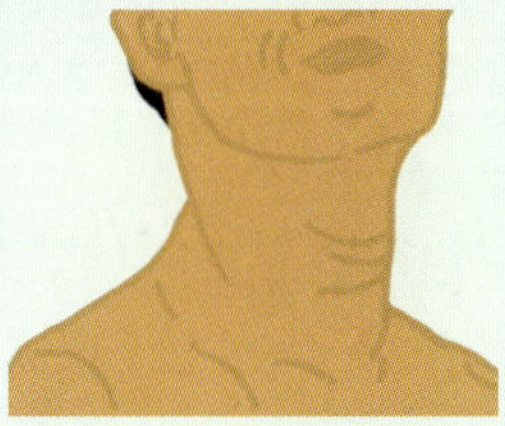

galoo گلو

thumb

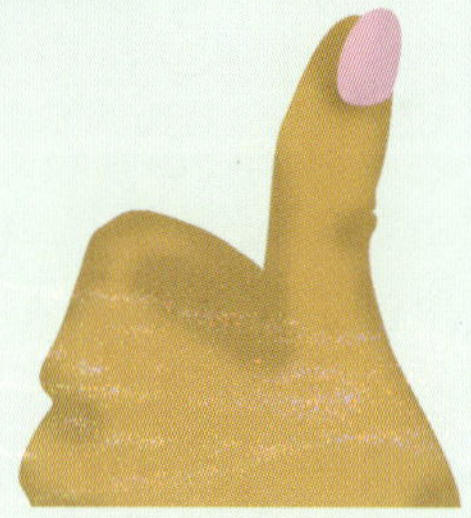

shast شست

ticket

bileet بلیط

tiger

babr ببر

toe

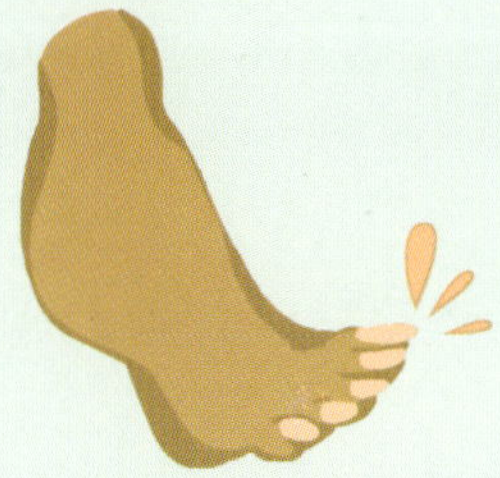

panje pa پنجه

tofu

خمیرسویا
khamir soya

tomato

گوجه فرنگی
goje farangee

tongue

zaban زبان

tool

abzar ابزار

toothbrush

mesvak مسواک

toothpaste

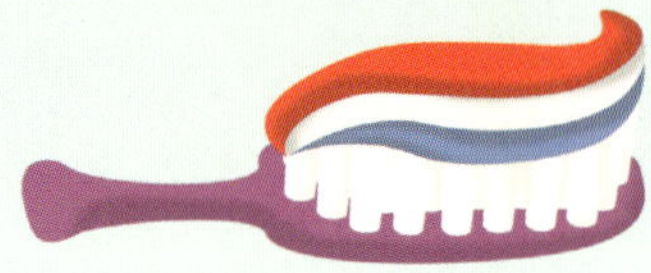

خمیر دندان
khamir dandan

tortoise

lakposht لاک پشت

towel

hol'e حوله

tower

borj برج

toy

اسباب بازی
asbabbazi

tractor

traktor تراکتور

train

ghatar قطار

tree

derakht درخت

triangle

mosallas مثلث

tub

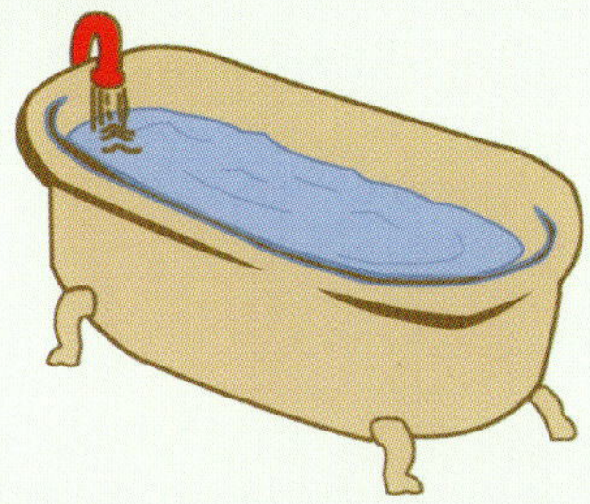

vaan وان

tunnel

toonel تونل

turnip

shalgham شلغم

tyre
US English **tire**

lastik لاستیک

Uu

umbrella

chatr چتر

uncle

amoo عمو

uniform

لباس فرم
lebase form

university

دانشگاه
daneshgah

utensil

وسایل آشپزی
vasayele ashpazee

a b c d e f g h i j k l m n o p q r s t u v w x y z

Vv

vacuum cleaner

جارو برقی
jaroo barghee

valley

darre دره

van

ماشین ون
mashine van

vase

goldan گلدان

vault

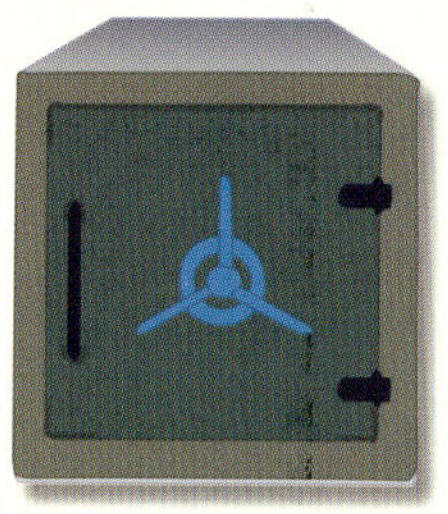

tagh طاق

vegetable

sabzee سبزی

veil

hajab حجاب

vet

دامپزشک
daam pezeshk

village

dehkade دهکده

violet

banafsh بنفش

violin

vialon ویولن

volcano

آتشفشان
atashfeshan

volleyball

valibal واليبال

vulture

karkas کرکس

Ww

waist

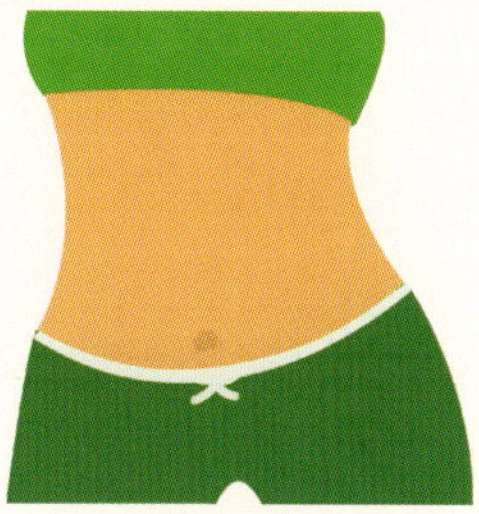

doare kamar دور کمر

waitress

پیشخدمت زن
pishkhedmate zan

wall

divar دیوار

wallet

kif pool کیف پول

walnut

gerdoo گردو

wand

gorz گرز

wardrobe

ja rakhty جا رختی

warehouse

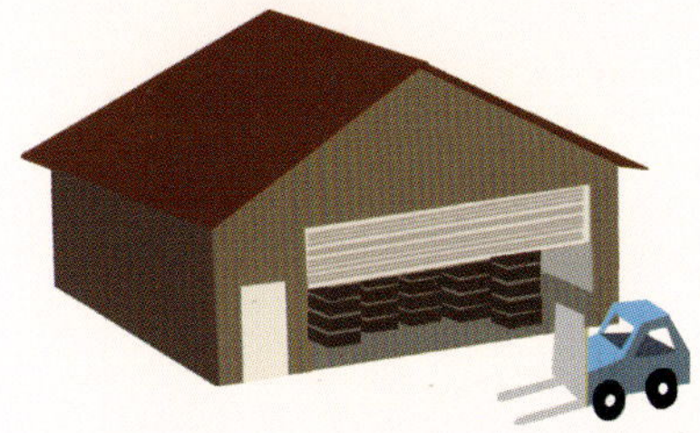

anbar انبار

wasp

زنبور بي عسل
zanboore bee asal

watch

saa'at ساعت

water

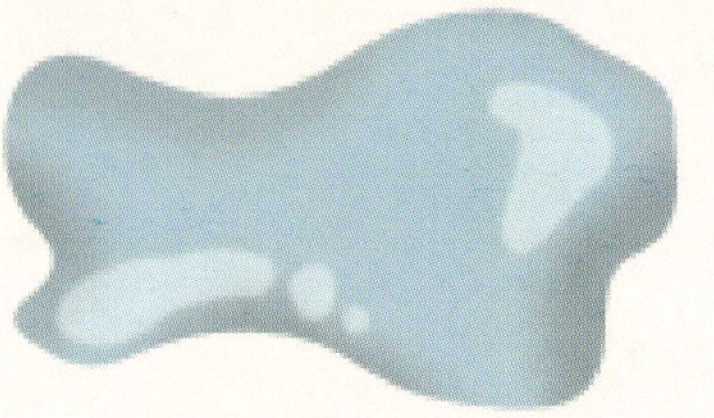

ab اب

watermelon

hendevane هندوانه

web

تارعنكبوت
tare ankaboot

whale

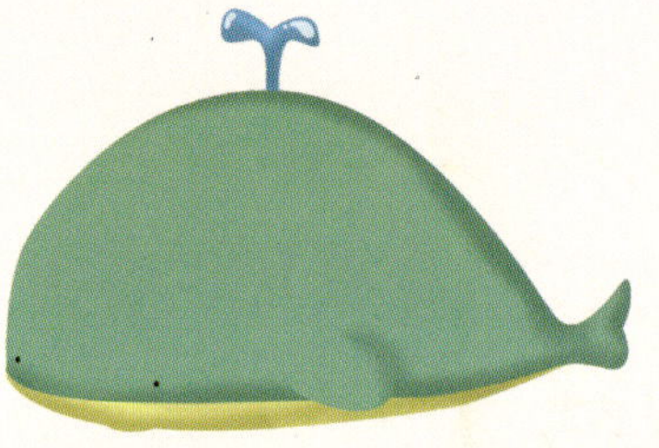

nahang نهنگ

wheat

gandoom گندم

wheel

charkh چرخ

whistle

soot سوت

white

safeed سفيد

wife

zan زن

window

panjere پنجره

wing

bal بال

winter

zemestan زمستان

wizard

jadoogar جادوگر

wolf

gorg گرگ

woman

zan زن

woodpecker

darkoob دارکوب

wool

pashm پشم

workshop

kargah کارگاه

wrist

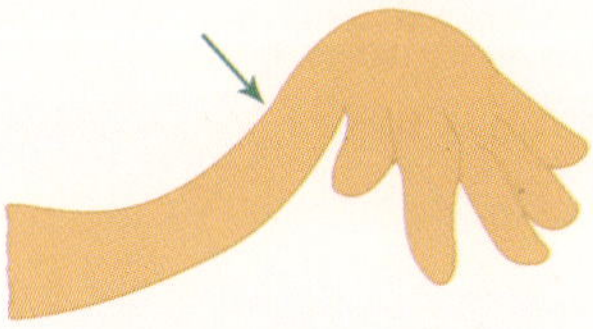

مچ دست

moche dast

Xx

x-ray

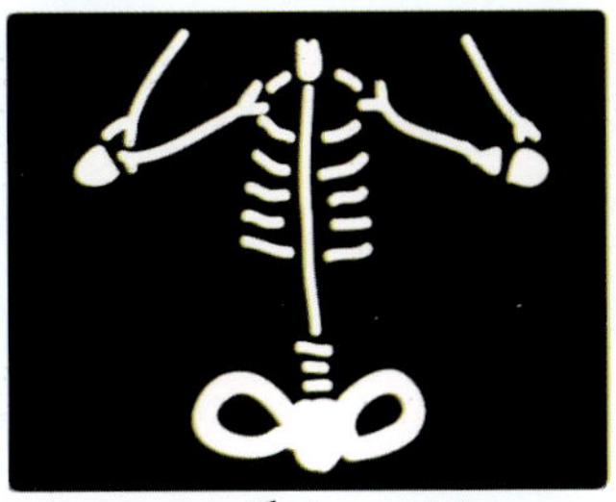

اشعه ایکس

ashae eex

xylophone

سنتور چوبی

santore chobee

a b c d e f g h i j k l m n o p q r s t u v w x y z

Yy

yacht

قایق بادبانی

qayq badbany

yak

گاو نر و کوهان دار

gave nar va kohandar

yard

hayat حیاط

yellow

rangzard رنگ زرد

yoghurt

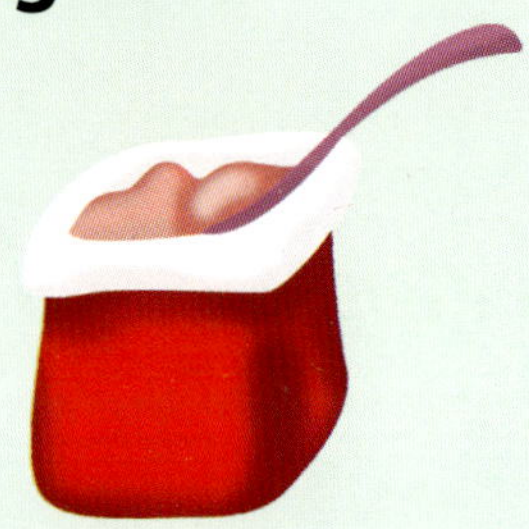

mast ماست

Zz

zebra

gorkhr گورخر

zero

sefr صفر

zip

زیپ لباس

zeepe lebas

zodiac

دایره البروج

dayere o'l borooj

zoo

باغ وحش

baghevahsh